SEVEN NEIGHBORHOODS IN
DETROIT
Recipes from the City

SEVEN NEIGHBORHOODS IN
DETROIT
Recipes from the City

J.N. CAMERON

AUBERGINE
BOOKS

For ordering information contact Beneva Publishing.
www.benevapublishing.com

Publisher's Cataloging-in-Publication Data

Cameron, J. N.
  Seven neighborhoods in Detroit : recipes from the city / J.
N. Cameron.
     pages cm
  Includes bibliographical references and index.
  ISBN: 978-0-9966261-0-1 (pbk.)
  ISBN: 978-0-9966261-1-8 (e-book)
  1. Cooking, American. 2. Food habits—Michigan—
Detroit—History. 3. Cooking—Michigan—Detroit—
History. 4. Detroit (Mich.)—Social life and customs. 5.
Cookbooks.   I. Title.
GT2853.U5   C36   2015
641.59774—dc23
                                        2015914395

First Edition

To my family in Michigan, my supportive husband, and homesick Detroiters everywhere – without them this book wouldn't have been possible.

CONTENTS

CONTENTS

INTRODUCTION

T his cookbook takes a nostalgic look at Detroit's most iconic dishes. It's people and local agriculture set the foundation from which these foods emerged. With popular dishes that range from baklava to pierogi, the influence of its first residents is undeniable.

But as any city evolves, so does its cuisine. Most ingredients are globally available and today recipes are developed without geographic limitations. This well-timed collection captures significant moments in food history and the cities most remarkable dishes to date.

THE NEIGHBORHOODS

By 1925, nearly half of Detroit's population was born outside of the United States.[1] Many spoke the universal language of food to make their new surroundings work. Some shared the meals of their homeland, often altering recipes to suite local tastes, or because traditional ingredients were unavailable. Others put their own spin on classic dishes or created new ones.

Each chapter tells the story of one neighborhood. And while some communities still thrive, others can only live on through stories...and their most celebrated dishes.

THE RECIPES

Recipes range from popular international dishes to genuine Detroit originals. They're simplified when possible so that cooks at any skill level can enjoy this book. Each recipe attempts to capture the specific essence of a dish, but feel free to modify any recipe to suit your tastes and dietary preferences.

THE INGREDIENTS

Michigan is abundant with livestock and agriculture. With more than eleven-thousand inland lakes (not to mention thirty-six thousand miles of rivers and streams), the state is teaming with freshwater fish too.

The following table illustrates a range of ingredients that are typical of the region. They are either Michigan-produced on a large scale or imported due to high-demand.

GREAT LAKES WILD RICE

Wild Rice is important to many tribal communities and is part of an ancient prophesy that brought the Ojibwa, Pottawatomi, and Odawa people to the region. The rice, called Manoomin in the Ojibwe culture, grows on water and is still hand-harvested by canoe.

At one time, vast rice beds grew along the shorelines and streams. But invasive plants and human impact have caused a serious decline in growth. The threatened species is tremendously important to the biodiversity of Michigan's waters.[2]

VEGETABLES	FRUIT	MEAT & POULTRY	SEAFOOD
sweet corn	apples	beef	trout
potatoes	cherries	pork	perch
cabbage	blueberries	turkey	herring
asparagus	strawberries	chicken	salmon
beets		game meat	smelt
wild mushrooms		(esp. venison)	whitefish
(esp. morels, oyster		Sausage	catfish
mushrooms)		(esp. kielbasa, natural-	
		casing hotdogs)	

CHEESE	GRAINS	PICKLED & FERMENTED	MISCELLANEOUS
Gouda	sweet corn		maple syrup
Muenster	wheat	sauerkraut	nuts
Swiss	wild rice	pickled beets	(esp. English walnuts,
Pinconning (colby-		pepperoncini	hazelnuts, chestnuts,
style cheese)		green olives	pistachios*)
cheddar		dill pickles*	
			*Detroit's Germack
Michigan's production		*Vlasic® is from	Pistachio Company is
of dairy products		Detroit	the oldest pistachio
ranks it #2 among all			roaster in the U.S.
states.			

THE FUTURE

Detroit was built on innovation. For self-starters with open-minds and a do-it-yourself mindset, even today the area offers endless opportunity. Its emerging food scene of artisan cheese makers, bakers, chefs, barbecue pit masters, and craft brewers, illustrates the true spirit of the city.

1 Arthur M Woodford, "A City of Many Tongues," In This Is Detroit, 1701-2001, (Detroit: Wayne State University Press, 2001), 186.
2 "Native Wild Rice Coalition," Native Wild Rice, (accessed September 28, 2015); available from http://www.nativewildricecoalition.com/native-wild-rice-coalition.html.

LITTLE ITALY
CHAPTER 1

Italians have contributed to the growth of Detroit for nearly three-hundred fifty years. It began with the arrival of Alphonso Tonti. He was second-in-command to the French explorer Antoine Cadillac. Together they founded Fort Pontchartrain du Détroit in 1701. With the arrival of their wives, they became the first European families to reside in the new territory.

Since the French and English discouraged immigration, the Italian population grew slowly. But after 1855, a steady migration began.[1] Then within the forty years spanning 1880 to 1920, several thousand Italians arrived from Sicily, Lombardy, and Genoa.

Some passed through on their way to work in the Upper Peninsula's mines. But many were there to stay. And though the Italian community no longer has a cultural center, like Mexicantown, there was once a *Little Italy* near Eastern Market.[2]

The original Farmer's Market opened downtown in 1841. Soon additional markets were built, including Eastern Market, which mainly sold hay and wood. But with the construction of sales sheds in 1891, it became a farmers market that sold produce and other goods.

Shortly before the expansion, Detroit's oldest Italian restaurant began to serve hot meals steps away from the market. The Marazza family offered room and board to vendors from out of town. Mrs. Marazza's reputation as a fine cook spread quickly. And with the encouragement of her patrons, she opened the Roma Café in 1890.[3]

Throughout the twentieth century, the manufacturing industry expanded and the Italian population grew. By 1925, there were forty-two thousand Italians in the city. Aside from their contributions to the automotive work force, many worked with stone, cement, and tile. Others were entrepreneurs who opened shops and restaurants.

They didn't stay contained in a *Little Italy*. They integrated into the diverse communities of southeast Michigan. Many of the Italians who initially settled near Eastern Market, went on to live in the northeastern suburbs, especially Macomb County. It is there that a myriad of Italian bakeries, groceries, and other businesses still thrive, despite competition from large supermarket chains. There are currently three hundred thousand Italian Americans in Metropolitan Detroit.

1 Armando Delicato, Italians in Detroit, (Charleston, SC: Arcadia, 2005).
2 "The "Little Italies" of Michigan," Jovina Cooks Italian, May 10, 2013, (accessed April 29, 2015); available from http://jovinacooksitalian.com/2013/05/10/the-little-italies-of-michigan/.
3 "History," Roma Café, (accessed April 29, 2015); available from http://www.romacafe.com/History.

MINESTRONE SOUP

Several Italian restaurants in southeast Michigan claim that minestrone soup is their specialty. Elegant, yet underappreciated, minestrone celebrates the freshest produce of the season. This recipe was inspired by a local variation, which at one time could be enjoyed downtown on Woodward Avenue.

Aromatics:
2 tablespoons extra-virgin olive oil
1 onion, diced
2 stalks celery, diced
1 large carrot, diced
pinch salt
2 teaspoons minced garlic
2 tablespoons tomato paste

Vegetables:
4 cups (32-ounces) chicken or vegetable stock
2 (14.5-ounce) cans stewed tomatoes, with liquid
1½ cups potato, diced
1 cup green beans, cut into 1-inch pieces
1 cup zucchini, diced
⅓ cup peas
⅓ cup corn
1 cup frozen spinach
½ cup uncooked pearl barley
½ cup cooked garbanzo beans
1 (15.5-ounce) can cooked cannellini beans, drained

Finishing Touches:
2 tablespoons fresh parsley, minced
1 teaspoon dried basil (or 1 tablespoon fresh basil, minced)
¼ teaspoon black pepper
salt, to taste
½ cup elbow macaroni, uncooked
½ cup heavy cream (optional)
¼ cup Parmigiano-Reggiano or other hard Italian cheese, grated (garnish)

1. Warm the oil in a heavy soup pot. Stir in the onions, celery, carrots, and a pinch of salt. Cover and sweat the vegetables over medium-low heat for about 10 minutes.

2. Remove the lid and stir in the garlic and tomato paste. Cook for a few minutes.

3. Stir in the chicken stock, tomatoes, vegetables, barley, and beans. Bring to a boil, then reduce the heat to medium-low. Cover and simmer for 1 hour. Add additional water or stock as needed.

4. Use an immersion blender or counter-top blender to purée half the soup. Return the puréed soup to the pot if using a counter-top blender.

5. Stir in the herbs, seasonings, and macaroni. Cook for another 30 minutes or until the pasta is cooked. Stir in the cream if using.

To serve:
Ladle into soup bowls and garnish with freshly grated Italian cheese.

ANTIPASTO SALAD

The first course of an Italian meal, *antipasto* in fact means "before the meal". Cured meats, cheeses, pepperoncini, olives, and other items are traditionally served from a platter. Detroiter's embrace this concept, but in the form of a salad tossed with a light vinaigrette. You may find it in proper Italian restaurants, but it's best served with Detroit-style square pizza.

Vinaigrette:
½ cup red wine vinegar
1 cup extra-virgin olive oil
2 teaspoons dried oregano
1 teaspoon minced garlic
1 teaspoon dried parsley
1 teaspoon dried basil
ground black pepper, to taste
salt, to taste

Salad:
1 head iceberg lettuce, chopped
½ pound sliced ham, cut into 1-inch squares
½ pound sliced salami, cut into 1-inch squares
1 cup cherry tomatoes, halved
8-ounces mild Wisconsin brick cheese, Monterey Jack, or provolone, cut or shredded
½ cup sliced black olives
pepperoncini (for serving)

1. Place the vinaigrette ingredients into a container with a lid. Shake vigorously until combined.

2. Mix the salad in a large bowl. Toss with vinaigrette just before serving. Garnish with whole or sliced pepperoncini.

DETROIT SQUARE PIZZA

Detroiters love pizza. In fact four of the nations top pizza chains began here: Dominos, Little Caesars, Hungry Howies, and Jet's Pizza. Local chains like Shields, Buscemi's, Buddy's, and several others have been around for ages, each with a passionate fanbase. There are also countless standalone pizzerias that feed the region.

We even have our very own regional style. Its creation is often credited to "Gus" Guerra, the owner of Buddy's Rendezvous on Conant, which was at one time a blind pig. It was first introduced as a new menu item in 1946.

Based on a Sicilian crust, Detroit-style pizza is built in reverse order, starting with pepperoni, then a generous sprinkling of cheese. Finally, rich tomato sauce is ladled over top. Its deep-dish crust is baked twice which results in a golden edge of crispy cheese.

But the secret ingredient may be the unique pan that they're baked in. During the manufacturing boom of the forties, square *blue steel* pans were used by factories to hold small parts on the production line. Though they were never meant for baking, local pizza chefs found that once seasoned, they captured flavor much like cast-iron. Blue Steel pans caught on and are still used to make authentic Detroit-style pizza today.

Makes two 8x10-inch rectangular pizzas

Dough:
1 cup warm water
2¼ teaspoons instant or active dry yeast
2 teaspoons granulated sugar
2 tablespoons vegetable oil
1 teaspoon salt
3 cups (385 grams) all-purpose flour

Assembly:
4 tablespoons vegetable oil (to oil the pan)
sliced pepperoni
1½ cups shredded low-moisture mozzarella cheese
1½ cups mild Wisconsin brick cheese, shredded or chopped (sub. Muenster or Italian blend)
your choice of toppings
pizza sauce

1. Start the pizza dough the night before like the professionals. In a small bowl, combine the warm water, yeast and sugar. Let the yeast activate for about 10 minutes *(You do not need to activate instant yeast)*. Stir in the oil and salt.

2. Place the flour into a large mixing bowl. Weigh the flour for the most accuracy.

3. Pour the yeast mixture into the flour. If needed, use a rubber spatula to scrape the salt and sugar from the bowl. Stir with a wooden spoon until the ingredients form a cohesive dough ball.

4. Place the dough into an oiled bowl and cover with plastic wrap. Let it cold-rise overnight in the refrigerator to develop flavor.

5. Remove the dough from the refrigerator. Leave it on the counter for about an hour to warm up.

6. For two 8x10-inch pizzas, divide the dough into two equal-sized pieces. Knead for a few minutes and shape into two balls. Cover with plastic wrap and let rest for 15 minutes. *(If only making one pizza, wrap one of the dough balls in plastic wrap and freeze.)*

7. Spread two tablespoons of vegetable oil onto each pan. Press the dough all the way to the sides of the pan, but don't form an edge like a regular crust. Press with your fingers to form a bumpy surface texture. *(If the dough is difficult to work with, set it aside for 10 minutes to relax the gluten.)*

8. Preheat the oven to 500°F. Cover the prepared dough with plastic wrap and let rise for another 30 minutes.

9. Before adding the toppings, pre-bake the crust for 10 minutes. Remove when slightly golden. Let rest for 5 minutes. Lower the oven-temperature to 400°F so the cheesy edges don't burn.

10. Assemble the pizzas. First add a layer of pepperoni. Combine the cheese and sprinkle an even layer all the way to the edges. Place additional toppings over the cheese. Bake for another 10 minutes or so.

11. Simmer the pizza sauce in a small saucepan. Ladle a few streaks of sauce over the pizza, but don't spread it to the edges. Bake for another 10 minutes.

Cut into large rectangles and serve with antipasto salad.

BAKED MOSTACCIOLI

Mostaccioli, which means "little mustaches" in Italian, is a casserole that is especially popular in the Midwest. The pasta dish with ground beef, tomato sauce, and gooey melted cheese is perfect for large gatherings. If you *do* have leftovers, which is unlikely, it's one of those meals that tastes even better the next day.

Sauce:
2 tablespoons extra-virgin olive oil
1½ pounds lean ground beef
½ teaspoon salt
1 small onion, diced
2 teaspoons minced garlic
1 cup sliced mushrooms (optional)
1 cup zucchini (optional)
1 (28-ounce) jar tomato sauce
½ cup water
1 bay leaf
ground black pepper, to taste

Assembly:
1 tablespoon salt (for boiling water)
1 pound uncooked mostaccioli pasta (substitute penne or ziti)
1 cup (8-ounces) grated Parmesan-style cheese
2 cups (16-ounces) shredded mozzarella cheese

1. Preheat the oven to 350°F and butter a 13x9-inch baking dish.

2. Heat the oil in a heavy-gauge pot over medium-high heat. Stir in the ground beef and salt. Break it up with a spatula and cook until browned. Tilt the pan and scoop out any excess grease.

3. Stir in the onion and cook until translucent. Add the garlic, mushrooms, and zucchini and cook for a few minutes longer.

4. Stir in the rest of the sauce ingredients and bring to a simmer. Lower the heat and cover the pot. Gently simmer for about 20 minutes. Stir occasionally.

5. Bring a pot of salted water to a rolling boil. Stir in the pasta and cook until *al dente*, or still slightly firm when bitten. Drain, but don't rinse. Reserve.

6. Taste the sauce and season to taste. Dispose of the bay leaf.

7. Combine the pasta with the sauce and pour the mixture into the baking dish. Cover with an even layer of Parmesan, then a layer of mozzarella cheese.

8. Cover loosely with foil and bake for 20 minutes. Remove the foil. Bake for another 20 minutes or until the cheese is lightly browned. Remove from the oven and let cool for 5 minutes before serving.

THREE-CHEESE MANICOTTI BAKE

In ancient times, dough was cut into large rectangles, stuffed with flavorful fillings, rolled then baked. *Manicotti* is one of the oldest types of pasta that is still prepared much like it was originally. This recipe features pasta filled with spinach and a blend of three Italian cheeses.

Cheese Filling:
2 cups ricotta cheese, drained
1 cup shredded low-moisture mozzarella cheese
¼ cup grated Parmigiano-Reggiano or Parmesan-style cheese
2 large eggs
½ cup frozen spinach, thawed and pressed to remove moisture
½ teaspoon black pepper
½ teaspoon salt
¼ teaspoon nutmeg

Assembly:
1 box manicotti or cannelloni pasta tubes
1 (28-ounce) jar tomato sauce
1½ cup shredded low-moisture mozzarella cheese
½ cup grated Parmigiano-Reggiano or Parmesan-style cheese
2 tablespoons butter, cut into small pieces

1. Combine the filling ingredients and refrigerate.

2. Preheat the oven to 375°F.

3. Bring a pot of salted water to a rolling boil. One at a time, add the pasta tubes and cook for about 8 minutes. Stir to make sure the pasta isn't sticking to the bottom of the pan. Drain, but don't rinse.

4. Spread half of the tomato sauce onto the bottom of a rectangular baking dish.

5. Scoop the cheese filling into a pastry bag or a plastic sandwich bag with a corner cut off. Squeeze the filling into each pasta tube and place into the baking dish. Pour the rest of the sauce over the manicotti.

6. Cover with foil and bake for 40 minutes. Remove the foil and top with both cheeses. Dot with bits of butter. Bake uncovered until the cheese is melted, about 15 minutes. Remove from the oven and let sit for 15 minutes before serving.

CRUSTY ITALIAN BREAD

Visitors may be amused by the way some local restaurants serve bread. Here it's not unusual to receive a bread basket with thick slices of warmed white bread in plastic sandwich bags. It's a great way for busy restaurant staff to prep bread in advance and keep it soft. Thick slices of Italian bread are perfect for any bread basket, with or without the plastic. This loaf is soft and fluffy with a crusty exterior.

Dough:
1¼ cups warm water
2¼ teaspoons instant yeast
2 teaspoons brown sugar
2 teaspoons kosher salt
1 tablespoon extra-virgin olive oil
3 cups (385 grams) all-purpose flour

For Baking:
cornmeal
1 egg white, lightly beaten
1 tablespoon sesame seeds

1. Combine the dough ingredients and mix well. Turn out onto a lightly floured surface and knead for 5 to 10 minutes. Transfer the dough to a large, oiled bowl. Cover with plastic wrap. Place in a warm area and let rise until double in size, about one hour.

2. Preheat the oven to 425°F. Dust a baking sheet with cornmeal.

3. Remove the plastic wrap and punch the dough to deflate. Turn out onto a lightly floured surface and flatten with the heel of your hand. Tightly roll the dough into an oval shape with tapered ends. Place it onto the baking sheet (or use a loaf pan). But don't cover it. Let rise for another 40 minutes or until double in size.

4. Make several diagonal slashes across the top of the dough with a sharp knife. Brush the dough with egg whites and sprinkle with sesame seeds.

5. Moisture is the key to a crusty exterior. Use a spray bottle to spray the loaf with water. Bake for three minutes. Open the oven door and spray again. Bake for another three minutes. Spray and bake one more time.

6. Bake for a final 30 to 40 minutes or until the crust is golden-brown. Let the bread cool for 10 minutes on a wire rack before slicing.

BAKED STROMBOLI

In the mid-1900s, Sicilian immigrants brought the concept of stromboli to the United States. It's based on the *bonata*, which loosely means "generous loaf".

To make stromboli, dough is rolled out, filled with a medley of meats, cheeses, vegetables and sometimes sauce. Then it's rolled into a spiral and baked until golden brown. Each slice reveals a spiral of savory fillings and melted cheese.

1 pound pizza dough *(recipe in chapter)*
1½ cups shredded low-moisture mozzarella cheese
1 tablespoon fresh parsley, minced
1 teaspoon dried oregano
½ teaspoon granulated garlic
6 ounces thinly sliced ham
6 ounces thinly sliced salami
additional toppings like mushrooms, green bell peppers, bacon, Italian sausage, fresh basil, spinach, jalapeños, pepperoncini, sliced black olives, marinara sauce ...the possibilities are endless.
4 ounces thinly sliced provolone cheese
extra-virgin olive oil

1. Preheat the oven to 375°F. On a lightly floured surface, roll the dough into a 12-inch rectangle.

2. Toss the mozzarella with the parsley, oregano, and garlic in a bowl. Sprinkle an even layer of the mixture over the dough.

3. Place a layer of ham, salami, then any additional toppings you want to use. Finally, top with the sliced provolone. Some ingredients, especially fresh mushrooms, should first be sautéed to release their moisture.

4. Roll the dough into a log beginning with the edge closest to you. Gently seal the ends as you roll forward. Lightly press to seal at the end.

5. Transfer the stromboli seam-side down onto a non-stick baking sheet. Brush the top with some olive oil or melted butter. Cover loosely with plastic wrap and let rise for about 30 minutes before baking.

6. Bake for 25 minutes or until golden brown.

To serve:
Cut the stromboli into thick spirals. Serve with marinara sauce or ranch dressing.

CANNOLI
Cannoli con Biancomangiare

A staple of Sicilian cuisine, cannoli are crunchy tube-shaped pastries that are filled with decadent creamy filling. Its ends are dipped into chopped nuts or chocolate bits, then they're dusted with powdered sugar. Most likely the Sicilians who settled in northeast Detroit introduced this delicacy to the area.

Unlike most American cities where cannoli are prevalent, we offer two kinds of filling. Sweet ricotta filling is the most well-known, but our cannoli are also filled with a creamy pudding called Biancomangiare. This type is also enjoyed in the ancient coastal town of Agrigento, which may be its origin.

Ricotta filling:
1 pound (2 cups) ricotta cheese, drained for at least 1 hour or overnight
½ cup caster sugar
2 teaspoons pure vanilla extract (or the seeds scraped from half of a vanilla bean)
½ teaspoon ground cinnamon
¼ teaspoon orange zest, minced (optional)
¼ cup miniature chocolate chips or grated chocolate

1. Mix the ingredients well and refrigerate until ready to use.

Biancomangiare 'pudding' filling:
1 liter (4¼ cups) half & half or whole milk
½ cup caster sugar
½ cup cornstarch
¼ teaspoon salt
½ teaspoon ground cinnamon
¼ teaspoon orange zest, minced
¼ cup miniature chocolate chips or grated chocolate

1. Except for the chocolate, whisk together the ingredients in a saucepan over medium heat.

2. Whisk constantly while it comes to a simmer. Just as it starts to thicken, remove the pan from the heat. Whisk vigorously until the pudding is thick. To thicken more, momentarily place the pan back over the heat and whisk. It will thicken even more as it cools.

3. Pour the custard into a bowl. Cover the surface directly with plastic wrap to prevent it from forming a skin. Refrigerate for at least four hours or overnight. When ready to use, whisk the custard until smooth. Stir the miniature chocolate chips or chocolate shavings into the cold custard.

CANNOLI (cont'd)

Cannoli Shells:
2 cups all-purpose flour
1 tablespoon granulated sugar
¼ teaspoon salt
2 tablespoons unsalted butter, cut into small pieces
1 egg yolk
¼ cup sweet Marsala wine or dry white wine
1 egg white, lightly beaten (to seal)
lard or oil (for frying)

Special Equipment:
metal cannoli tubes or heavy duty foil rolled into tubes (for frying)

1. Sift together the flour, sugar and salt in a mixing bowl. With your fingertips (or a pastry blender), work the butter pieces into the flour until the mixture feel like coarse grains. Stir in the wine and egg yolk to form a smooth dough.

2. Wrap the dough in plastic wrap and let it rest at room temperature for at least 30 minutes.

3. Roll out the dough on a lightly floured surface to about ⅛-inch thick. Cut the dough into 5-inch circles or ovals.

4. Loosely wrap each circle around the cannoli tubes. Wet the edges with beaten egg white and press gently to seal.

5. Line a large baking dish with paper towels to absorb excess oil after frying.

6. In a heavy pot, bring a few inches of oil to 375°F.

7. Fry two or three at a time in the hot oil. Turn with tongs to fry evenly on all sides. Carefully remove and place onto the paper towel to cool.

8. After about 10 minutes the cannoli will be cool enough to remove from the tubes. Store uncovered at room temperature if not filling immediately.

Assembly:
cannoli shells (home-made or purchased)
ricotta or custard filling
garnish - miniature chocolate chips, grated chocolate, sliced almonds or chopped pistachios
confectioners sugar

1. Fill just before serving so that the shells stay crisp. Fill a pastry bag or use a plastic sandwich bag with one end cut off. Pipe some filling into one end of the shell, filling halfway. Then fill the other end. Repeat with the rest of the shells.

2. Sprinkle or dip each end into your favorite garnish. Dust a layer of confectioners sugar over the finished cannoli. Enjoy!

AMERICAN GOULASH

Many Detroiters grew up eating this satisfying one-pot meal. An everyday supper in the Midwest, goulash is easy and economical for anyone on a budget. The oldest known recipe was found in the *Cookbook of the Woman's Educational Club* from 1914[1]. There are many versions today, but the core ingredients are always beef, pasta, and tomatoes.

1 pound elbow macaroni
1 tablespoon vegetable oil
2 pounds lean ground beef
1 medium onion, chopped
1 large green bell pepper, diced (optional)
1 teaspoon minced garlic
½ teaspoon salt
½ teaspoon black pepper
1 teaspoon paprika
1 (15-ounce) can tomato sauce
1 (28-ounce) can stewed tomatoes with juice
1 cup water
pinch red pepper flakes (or a splash of hot sauce)
1 cup shredded cheese of your choice (for serving)

1. First, prepare the macaroni (al dente) according to the instructions on its package. Set aside.

2. In a large pot, heat the oil and brown the ground beef. Break it into chunks as it cooks.

3. Stir in the onion, green bell pepper, and minced garlic. Sprinkle with the salt. Lower the heat and cover. Sweat the vegetables for 10 minutes.

4. Remove the lid and stir in the black pepper, paprika, tomatoes, water and red pepper flakes. Bring to a boil, then adjust the heat to low. Cover and simmer for 10 minutes. Stir occasionally.

5. Add the macaroni. Cover and cook for a few more minutes.

To serve:
Ladle into soup bowls and top with shredded cheese. Leftover goulash tastes even better the next day. So don't forget to refrigerate the leftovers.

1 Woman's Educational Club of Toledo, Ohio, Cookbook of the Woman's Educational Club (Toledo, OH, 1914), 49.

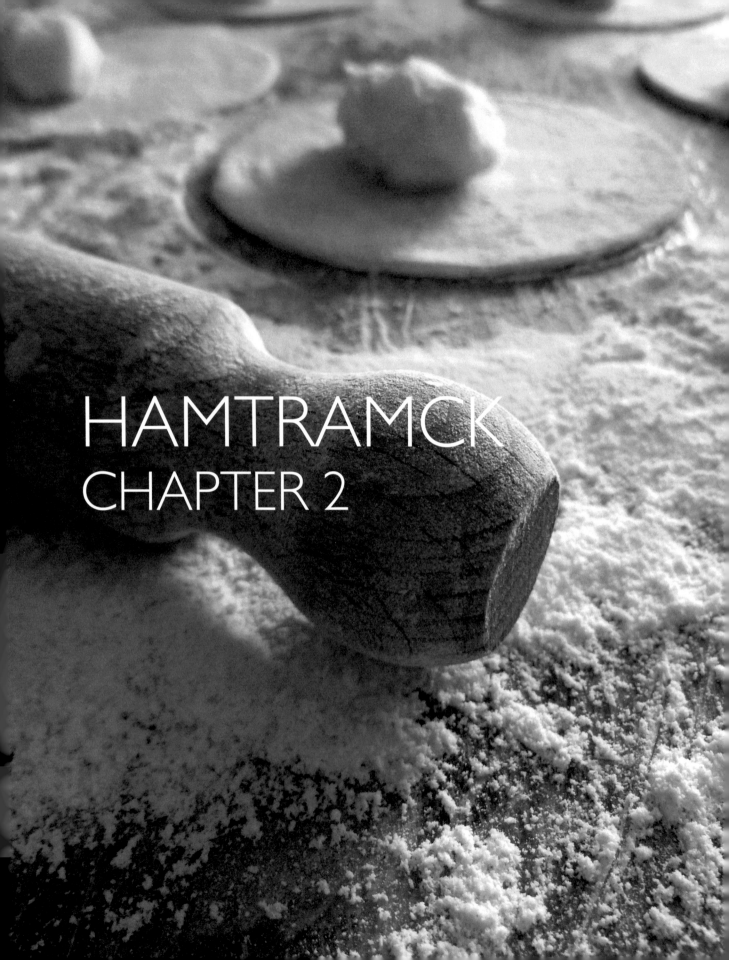

HAMTRAMCK
CHAPTER 2

Detroit's Polish community remained within Poletown and Hamtramck for many years. The neighborhoods were cultural hubs, with Polish newspapers, businesses, social activities, and organizations. But the heart of the community was its church. Over three hundred families organized St. Albertus Parish. Then in 1871, they built St. Albertus Roman Catholic Church at St. Aubin and Canfield Avenue. They kept their cultural identity strong by adapting their traditions, language, and faith.[1]

The late nineteenth century was a time of great economic change. Detroit began to transition from a commerce based economy to one driven by manufacturing. A strong infrastructure was essential to accommodate the new industry. And with only four paved roads in 1887, a strong workforce was needed to build new roads and railways. Industrialization provided many opportunities.

In 1914, the Dodge Brothers began to build the Dodge Main plant in Hamtramck. As a result, an influx of Polish laborers entered the area seeking employment. By 1925, Detroit had 115,000 Polish residents, and over 50,000 of them called Hamtramck home.

Their influence on local gastronomy is unmistakable. Poland's rich farmland produces abundant yields of potatoes, cabbage, and beets. From these crops came classic dishes like beet soup, stuffed cabbage, potato pancakes, and pierogi. Their comforting cuisine was a natural fit in the cold climate of Detroit.

Though the area remains exceedingly international, much of the Polish population has moved on to the suburbs. It's not the Polish enclave it once was, but its renowned Polish restaurants, bakeries, and bars still thrive. Kowalski Sausage Company,[2] New Palace Bakery, Polish Village Cafe, Polonia, and many others still churn out amazing food just as they have for ages.

Today the Poles are the second largest ethnic group in Michigan. With a population of 850,000, they're the third largest in the country, behind New York and Illinois.[3]

1 United States. National Park Service, "St. Albertus Catholic Church." National Parks Service (accessed September 4, 2015); available from http://www.nps.gov/nr/travel/detroit/d9.htm.
2 "The Kowalski Story" (accessed September 4, 2015); available from http://www.kowality.com/category-s/124.htm.
3 "Bentley Historical Library | University of Michigan," Polish Americans in Michigan, (accessed April 29, 2015); available from http://bentley.umich.edu/legacy-support/poles/.

DILL PICKLE SOUP

This unique soup is easy to find in Hamtramck, and even easier to make yourself. The briny zip of pickles is balanced with comforting vegetables and sour cream.

2 tablespoons unsalted butter
1 medium onion, diced
2 medium carrots, shredded
1 teaspoon salt
2 large potatoes, peeled and diced
1 cup dill pickles, finely chopped
6 cups chicken stock
1 cup all-purpose flour
1 cup water
1 cup sour cream
pickle juice, to taste
salt and pepper, to taste

Garnish:
fresh parsley, minced
fresh dill, minced

1. Warm the vegetable oil in a heavy pot over medium-high heat. Stir in the onion and carrots. Sprinkle with salt. Adjust the heat to medium-low, then cover with a lid. Sweat the vegetables for 10 minutes to release their flavor.

2. Stir in the potatoes, pickles, and chicken stock. Bring to a boil, then reduce the heat to low. Cover and simmer for 30 minutes.

3. Whisk the flour, water, and sour cream together in a bowl. While whisking the hot soup, very slowly add the mixture to avoid curdling.

4. Cook for a few minutes over medium heat until the soup has thickened slightly.

5. Taste the soup. Stir in pickle juice, salt, and pepper to taste. Serve immediately.

To Serve:
Ladle into soup bowls. Garnish with fresh parsley and dill.

POTATO PANCAKES
Placki Ziemniaczane

Potato pancakes have a place in many cuisines throughout Europe. During the mid-nineteenth century, a series of failing crops led to a mass-planting of potatoes in Poland and the Ukraine. They were easy and economical to grow.

Potato pancakes were often a substitute for bread during times of economic difficulty. They were a food staple in Polish monasteries in the seventeenth century. Called *Latkes* in Yiddish, they're also an Ashkenazi Jewish tradition, especially during Hanukkah.

3 cups potatoes, grated
2 eggs
¼ cup onion, minced
1 teaspoon baking soda
½ teaspoon salt
½ teaspoon ground black pepper
¼ cup all-purpose flour
vegetable oil (for frying)

1. Place grated potatoes into a strainer over a bowl. Press the potatoes to expel excess moisture.

2. Whisk together the eggs, onions, baking soda, salt, and pepper in a mixing bowl.

3. Stir in the potatoes and gently fold in the flour to form a thick batter.

4. Place 1 tablespoon of vegetable oil into a large non-stick frying pan over medium heat. When the oil is hot, spoon some batter into the pan. Spread to form a pancake. You may be able to fit 2 or 3 at a time. But, don't overcrowd the pan. Fry on each side until brown, about 3 minutes per side.

5. Place the cooked pancakes onto a paper towel lined plate to absorb excess oil. Repeat with the rest of the batter.

To serve:
Top the hot pancakes with meat sauce, goulash, sour cream, apple sauce, cottage cheese, or fruit syrup.

CUCUMBERS IN SOUR CREAM
Mizeria

This traditional peasant dish became known as Mizeria, meaning misery. But this cool and creamy salad is far from miserable.

Cucumber Prep:
2 large English cucumbers, sliced thin
salt

Dressing:
1 cup sour cream
1 tablespoon white vinegar
2 tablespoons fresh dill, chopped
¼ cup chives or scallions, sliced (optional)
ground black pepper, to taste

1. Salt the cucumbers liberally and place them into a paper towel lined strainer set over a bowl. Refrigerate for 30 minutes to an hour.

2. Wipe excess salt from each slice with a paper towel. Squeeze out the remaining moisture. Pat the cucumbers dry. Place them into a clean bowl and refrigerate until ready to serve.

3. Whisk together the dressing ingredients in a small bowl. Just before serving, toss the cucumbers with the dressing. Garnish with sprigs of fresh dill.

HOMEMADE KRAUT

All you need is cabbage, salt, and a little patience, to make sauerkraut from scratch. It's loaded with vitamins, minerals and has more beneficial lactobacillus bacteria than even yogurt. Sauerkraut is great with kielbasa, pierogi, and stuffed cabbage.

2 large heads white cabbage
¼ cup non-iodized salt
large crock or container (glass or enamel coated)
2 large plastic zipper storage bags

More salt will produce sauerkraut that is crunchier and lasts longer. Less salt makes softer sauerkraut.

1. Sanitize the utensils and container in a dishwasher or with boiling water.

2. Discard the cabbages outer leaves. Slice very thinly or use a food processor.

3. Place alternating layers of cabbage and salt into the container.

4. With very clean hands or a wooden spoon, crush the cabbage until it begins to expel juice. Pack it down until the water level rises above the cabbage. It must be completely submerged.

5. Fill a large food-grade freezer bag with water. Seal it well. Then place it inside of another freezer bag. Close tightly to prevent leakage. Place the bag on top of the cabbage, covering the entire surface. Cover tightly with plastic wrap.

6. Store the container in an area that is between 70°F-75°F. The cabbage will begin to ferment within a day. Check for tartness after three weeks. Once fermented, it can be eaten immediately, stored in the refrigerate to slow fermentation, or frozen.

BEER BRAISED KIELBASA AND KRAUT

1 tablespoon vegetable oil
1 pound kielbasa sausage, cut into 1-inch pieces
2 teaspoons brown sugar
1 large onion, chopped
1 (32-ounce) jar silver-floss or home-made sauerkraut, rinsed with water
1 (12-ounce) can beer or chicken stock
1 large potato, diced (optional)
2 teaspoons caraway seeds (optional)

1. Place the vegetable oil into a frying pan over medium-high heat. Sauté the kielbasa, brown sugar, and onions, just until the onions begin to soften. Remove from the heat and set aside.

2. Rinse the sauerkraut with cold water. Place half into a crock pot or a heavy, non-reactive pot with a lid to cook on the stove.

3. Add a layer of potatoes, if using, then the kielbasa and onions. Top with the remaining sauerkraut and caraway seeds. Pour in the beer or chicken stock, then cover with a lid.

4. Cook over low heat for at least 2 hours. If cooking on the stove top, add water as needed and stir occasionally to prevent burning.

STUFFED CABBAGE
Golabki

Stuffed Cabbage is an ancient concept and there are many versions throughout Eastern Europe and the Middle East. In the United States, stuffed cabbage is easiest to find in areas with a significant Polish population. They're often served during holidays, weddings, and Polish family reunions.

1 medium cabbage
1 cup rice
1 cup water
1 large onion, chopped
3 tablespoons butter or margarine
1 pound lean ground beef
½ pound lean ground pork
1 large egg
¾ teaspoon salt
½ teaspoon granulated garlic
½ teaspoon onion powder
½ teaspoon paprika
½ teaspoon ground black pepper
½ teaspoon baking soda

Sauce:
3 cups tomato juice
1 cup water, beef or chicken stock

1. Prepare the cabbage leaves in advance. Remove the tough outer layers, then rinse and core the cabbage. Place in a plastic freezer bag and freeze. When ready to use, let the cabbage thaw. The leaves will peel off easily. Place a few at a time into boiling water to slightly soften. Remove from the water and strain. Let cool in the refrigerator.

2. Prepare the rice. Bring the rice and water to a boil in a pot. Once boiling, adjust the heat to low. Cover with a lid and cook undisturbed for 15 minutes. Remove from the heat and allow the rice to cool completely. Reserve.

3. Sauté the onions in butter until translucent. Set aside to cool.

4. In a mixing bowl, combine the cooled onion and rice with the raw meat, egg, salt, garlic, onion, paprika, black pepper, and baking soda.

5. Preheat oven to 350°F. Place a scoop of filling onto each leaf. Roll the leaf forward, tucking in the sides as you roll. Don't roll too tightly. Repeat with the remaining leaves. Place the cabbage rolls side by side in a baking dish or Dutch oven.

6. Make the sauce. Whisk the tomato juice with the water or stock. Pour over the rolls until they are covered. Cover with foil and bake for 1½ hours or until the meat is fully cooked.

To serve:
Place one or two cabbage rolls onto a plate and top with tomato sauce. Serve with mashed potatoes.

CITY CHICKEN

With roots in the midwestern and eastern industrial areas of the United States, City Chicken has been popular in Detroit for generations. Despite not actually being a Polish dish, it's easy to find in local Polish restaurants.

It's not actually chicken either. This working class meal evolved during the Great Depression when pork was more affordable than chicken. City Chicken features skewers of breaded pork and veal that are baked to perfection in a classic pan gravy.

1 pound lean beef or veal, cut into large cubes
1 pound lean pork, cut into large cubes
salt and freshly ground black pepper
1 cup all-purpose flour
2 large eggs, whisked
1 cup bread crumbs (plain or seasoned)
2 tablespoons vegetable oil

Gravy:
3 tablespoons butter or margarine
3 tablespoons all-purpose flour
1½ cups milk or chicken stock
freshly ground black pepper, to taste
salt, to taste

Special Equipment:
6 Skewers

1. Preheat the oven to 325°F. Lightly dust the cubes of meat with salt and pepper. Alternating the pork and beef, place five cubes onto each skewer.

2. Prepare three plates. Spread flour across one plate, the eggs onto the second plate, then bread crumbs on the third. Roll each skewer in flour, coat with egg, then cover with bread crumbs. Refrigerate for 30 minutes.

3. In a large frying pan, heat the vegetable oil over medium-high heat. Use tongs to brown the meat skewers on all sides. Place the skewers into an oiled baking dish.

4. Melt the butter in the same pan used to fry the skewers. Whisk in the flour. While whisking vigorously, slowly pour in the milk or chicken stock. Cook for a few more minutes to thicken. Season with salt and freshly ground black pepper to taste.

5. Pour the gravy over the chicken. Cover loosely with foil and bake for 1½ hours. Uncover for the final 15 minutes of cooking time. Remove from the oven and serve.

To serve:
Serve city chicken with mashed potatoes, sauerkraut, and steamed vegetables.

POTATO & CHEDDAR PIEROGI

Though pierogi are historically considered peasant food, they're so irresistible that even Poland's elite grew to appreciate them. The half-moon shaped dumplings are stuffed with fillings like mashed potatoes, cheese, ground meat, sauerkraut, mushrooms, or fruit.

Hand-crafting pierogi can be time consuming, but they're worth the effort. And they freeze well, so make a double or triple batch to enjoy throughout the year.

Makes about three dozen

Potato & Cheddar Filling:
3 large potatoes, peeled and roughly chopped
½ cup (4-ounces) to 1 cup (8-ounces) shredded sharp cheddar cheese
salt and black pepper, to taste
2 tablespoons fresh chives, minced (optional)

Dough:
1 cup water
½ teaspoon salt
3 tablespoons vegetable oil
2½ to 3 cups all-purpose flour (plus more for rolling out the dough)

1. Make the filling in advance. Boil the potatoes until soft. Drain. Mash well or purée with a food processor. Stir in the cheese while still hot. After the filling has slightly cooled, stir in the chives. Taste and season with salt and pepper. Cool completely in the refrigerate until ready to use.

2. Make the dough. Combine the water, salt, and oil in a large mixing bowl. Mix in enough flour to form a soft dough. Knead for a few minutes on a lightly floured surface. If the dough is too moist, knead a little more flour into it. Let rest for 10 minutes.

3. Assemble the pierogi. Roll the dough out thinly on a lightly floured surface. Dough that is too thin may tear open when assembling or boiling.

4. Cut circles into the dough using a round cutter or the rim of a drinking glass. Keep a small bowl of flour handy to dip the cutter between cuts. Otherwise, it will stick to the dough.

5. Depending on the size of the circle, place a small amount of filling onto one side of the circle leaving an edge. Don't overfill.

6. Pour some tap water into a small cup. Dip your finger or a brush into the water and moisten the edge that contains the filling. Fold the dough over the filling flush to the edge. Press the edge gently with the tines of a fork to seal. Repeat with the remaining circles.

7. Bring a pot of salted water to a boil. Drop a few pierogi at a time into the pot. Once they float to the top, remove with a slotted spoon. Place each pierogi onto a baking sheet lined with oiled parchment to prevent sticking.

To serve:
Bake or fry in butter until golden brown. Plate a few pierogi, then top with sour cream and chives or sautéed onions. Freeze extra pierogi until ready to eat.

PACZKI
Polish Jelly Doughnuts

Every year the entire Metro-Detroit area joins together to celebrate *pączki*. Hamtramck hosts its annual Pączki Day parade and bars throw all-day parties that start at sunrise.

Pączki, which means "little package" in Polish, are dense, jelly-filled doughnuts eaten the day before Lent. Their original purpose was to use up prohibited ingredients, like lard and eggs, before the forty-day fast observed by Roman Catholics.

Detroiters of all backgrounds celebrate Pączki Day by indulging in pączki from one of the areas long-standing Polish bakeries. Lines stretch far down the street and form as early as three in the morning. Customers wait for several hours, enduring frigid temperatures, to purchase pączki by the box-load.

Dough:
1½ cups warm milk
1 package (2¼ teaspoons) active dry yeast
½ cup (1 stick) butter, softened
½ cup granulated sugar
3 egg yolks
1 tablespoon rum or brandy (optional)
1 teaspoon orange zest
1 teaspoon salt
4½ cups all-purpose flour
lard or vegetable oil (for frying)

Glaze:
1½ cups (150 grams) confectioners sugar
3 to 4 tablespoons milk or water

Sugar Topping:
caster sugar or confectioners sugar

Filling:
Prepared custard, fruit jam, or lemon curd

PACZKI (cont'd)

1. Sprinkle yeast over the warm milk in a small bowl. Set aside for 10 minutes to activate the yeast.

2. In a large mixing bowl, cream together the softened butter and sugar until fluffy. Add the egg yolks, liquor, orange zest, and salt. Mix well.

3. Whisk in the yeast mixture. Then stir in the flour until it becomes a dough ball.

4. Place the dough into an oiled bowl and move to a warm area. Cover and let rise for about one hour or until double in size. Punch down to deflate. Form into a ball.

5. On a lightly floured surface, roll out the dough ¾-inch thick. Cut circles with a 3-inch round cutter dipped in flour. Re-roll the scraps. Place the circles onto a baking sheet. Cover and let rise in a warm place for about 30 minutes or until double in size.

6. Fry the circles in hot lard or vegetable oil at 375°F. The dough will float to the top. Cook for about 2 minutes on each side, flipping only once. Remove with a slotted spoon and place onto a paper towel lined plate to absorb the oil.

7. If you prefer a glazed pączki, whisk the sugar and liquid together. Pour it into a bowl. Press the warm pączki halfway into the glaze. Remove with your fingertips, then place it glaze-side up onto a wire rack to cool before filling. The glaze will drip down the sides of the warm pączki leaving a nice even coating of sweetness.

8. For a sugar coating, instead toss with caster sugar while warm.

9. To fill the pączki, use a pastry bag with a large tip. Poke a hole into its side and pipe a generous amount of filling into each pączki. (If you don't have a pastry bag, fill a plastic sandwich bag and cut off one corner. Use a utensil, like a chopstick, to first poke a hole, then fill the pączki.)

MICHIGAN SALAD

With apples, cherries, and maple syrup, this salad celebrates the best of Michigan agriculture. Apples are one of Michigan's largest and most valuable crops.[1] In the fall, locals travel to nearby orchards to nibble on cider and doughnuts, then take a *hayride* to pick apples by the bushel. *It's tradition!*

Michigan also produces about ninety thousand gallons of maple syrup annually.[2] And with 3.8 million tart cherry trees, Michigan produces up to 75 percent of the tart cherries grown in the United States.[3]

Maple Vinaigrette:
1 tablespoon Dijon mustard
1 tablespoon white wine vinegar
2 tablespoons maple syrup (substitute cherry or raspberry jam)
¼ cup extra-virgin olive oil
freshly ground black pepper
salt

Whisk the dressing ingredients together. Add black pepper and salt to taste. Reserve.

Salad:
1 head romaine lettuce
1 granny smith apple, cored and sliced
1 cup grilled chicken breast, sliced (optional)
½ cup dried cherries (preferably Michigan-grown Montmorency Tart Cherries)
¼ cup walnut halves, lightly toasted
¼ cup blue cheese, crumbled

1. Wash the romaine lettuce well and tear into bite-sized pieces. Place it into a large salad bowl.

2. Top the romaine with apple slices, grilled chicken, cherries, walnuts, and blue cheese. Toss with vinaigrette just before serving.

1 Cherry Industry, Traverse City, (accessed July 9, 2015); available from http://www.traversecity.com/area/about-traverse-city/cherry-industry/.
2 Michigan Apples, - Pure Michigan Travel, (accessed July 9, 2015); available from http://www.michigan.org/hot-spots/michigan-apples/.
3 Michigan Maple Syrup Facts, Michigan Maple Syrup Facts, (accessed July 9, 2015); available from http://www.michiganagriculture.com/foods/michigan-maple-syrup/.

MAURICE SALAD

Made famous by the J.L. Hudson's restaurant downtown, the Maurice Salad features sliced deli meat, sweet pickles, green olives, and eggs tossed with a creamy dressing.

The Hudson's building was a local treasure, and at one point the world's tallest department store. Then in 1998, Hudson's broke two more records. It was the largest (2.2 million square feet) and also the tallest (439 feet) building ever to be demolished by a controlled implosion.[1]

This recipe is adapted from "The Marshall Field's Cookbook".

Dressing:
1 cup mayonnaise
2 teaspoons white wine vinegar
2 teaspoons honey
2 teaspoons Dijon mustard
1 tablespoon fresh parsley, minced
1 tablespoon shallots, minced (substitute onion)
1 teaspoon fresh lemon juice
freshly ground black pepper
salt

1. Whisk the ingredients together in a bowl. Add the black pepper and salt to taste. Refrigerate until ready to use.

Salad:
4 cups (1 medium head) iceberg lettuce, shredded
½ pound (8-ounces) sliced ham, julienned (cut into thin strips)
½ pound (8-ounces) sliced turkey breast, julienned
½ pound (8-ounces) Swiss cheese, julienned
½ cup sweet gherkin pickles, chopped
2 hard-boiled eggs, chopped
½ cup pimento-stuffed green olives

To serve:
Portion the lettuce onto salad plates. Arrange the ham, turkey, cheese, pickles, eggs, and green olives over top. Serve the salad dressing on the side.

1 World Records, World Records, (accessed July 9, 2015); available from http://www.controlled-demolition.com/world-records.

CHINATOWN
CHAPTER 3

Today just a handful of Chinese immigrants call the Cass Corridor home, but it was once the site of a thriving Chinatown. It began in 1872 when the first Chinese resident, *Ah-Chee*, arrived from Canton. He opened a simple laundry business in a small, crudely built shack on Gratiot Avenue. Business flourished and before long his friend, Lu-How, and others arrived to help.[1]

It wasn't until thirty-three years later that the first two Chinese restaurants opened their doors. Both were simple lunch rooms that fed hungry sailors along the waterfront.

But when Chicago transplant, Homer Gam, opened *King Yink Lo*, he introduced Chinese food to the general public of Detroit.[2] Along with a newly discovered cuisine, diners experienced grand opening fireworks so spectacular that police rushed to the scene assuming the worst.

At its peak in the twenties, Chinatown had three-hundred laundry businesses and twelve Chinese restaurants. The oldest American-based producer of Asian food products, La Choy, was founded. And one of the most beloved figures in Chinatown's history, Harry Chung, moved into the area.

Called the 'Mayor of Chinatown', Chung often smoked a trademark black cigar. He founded and led the Chinese Merchants Association, and opened the iconic *Chung's Restaurant* on Third Avenue.

Then after almost ninety years, Chinatown was condemned by the Detroit Housing Commission. When alternate plans fell through, thousands of residents were left nearly homeless. Eventually, with the aid of the Chinese Merchants Association, a more prosperous Chinatown was developed about a mile North at Cass and Peterboro. The flashy new Chinatown featured neon lights, restaurants, mah jong parlors, laundries, and curio shops.

But before long, a gang of young Chinese immigrants called the *Fay Lung*, or 'Flying Dragons', began to extort money from local business owners. Merchants who didn't pay were threatened with death. While some business owners purchased guns and bulletproof vests, others fled to the suburbs instead. Intensifying violence and urban decline led to Chinatown's ultimate demise.

Although a historic road marker indicates the site of Chinatown, few Chinese American establishments still operate within the city. The MGM Grand Casino was built on the land where the original Chinatown once stood.[3]

1 Zia, Helen, Asian American Dreams: The Emergence of an American People, (New York: Farrar, Straus, and Giroux, 2001).
2 Asian Americans in Metro Detroit, U.S., Detroit Free Press, (accessed April 29, 2015);
3 Detroit Chinatown, Zuzindlak, Chelsea, (accessed April 29, 2015); available from http://www.detroitchinatown.org.

EGGDROP SOUP

Eggdrop soup is the perfect starter for a Chinese meal. And you'll love how easy it is to make this classic restaurant-style soup from scratch.

4 cups chicken stock
3 eggs, lightly beaten
¼ teaspoon white pepper
a few drops of sesame oil (optional)
3 tablespoons cornstarch
salt, to taste
2 scallions, thinly sliced (to garnish)

1. Lightly simmer the chicken stock in a pot.

2. While stirring in one direction, pour a thin stream of the eggs into the stock.

3. Stir in the white pepper and sesame oil (if using).

4. Mix the cornstarch with an equal amount of water. Stir the mixture into the stock. Briefly simmer over medium heat until slightly thickened.

5. Taste the soup and add salt if needed.

To serve:
Ladle the soup into bowls and garnish with sliced scallions. Serve hot.

BEAN SPROUT EGG ROLLS

You may have discovered that egg rolls outside of Metro-Detroit are loaded with cabbage. Where are the bean sprouts?! And why sprouts?

The answer may relate to the fact that the oldest American producer of Asian food products, La Choy, was founded in Detroit. Founders Ilhan New and Wally Smith launched their first product in 1922...canned bean sprouts!

Filling:
3 tablespoons vegetable oil
1 small yellow onion, minced
½ pound lean pork, chopped finely
1 teaspoon minced garlic
1 cup cabbage, shredded
½ cup carrot, grated
1 (8-ounce) can water chestnuts, finely chopped
1 (8-ounce) can bamboo shoots, finely chopped
1 tablespoon soy sauce
2 teaspoons sherry
½ teaspoon salt
¼ teaspoon white pepper
¼ teaspoon sugar
2 cups bean sprouts, rinsed and drained

*Prepare the filling in advance. Cool completely before assembling the egg rolls.

1. In a large pan or wok, heat the oil, then add the onions and pork. Stir-fry over medium-high heat until the pork is fully cooked.

2. Excluding the bean sprouts, mix in the rest of the filling ingredients. Stir-fry for about five minutes.

3. Stir in the bean sprouts. Cook just until they begin to soften, but don't overcook. Taste the filling and add more salt if needed.

4. Place the filling into a strainer over a large bowl to collect excess liquid. Press to expel as much moisture as possible. Cool completely in the refrigerator.

Assembly:
1 egg, lightly whisked
1 package egg roll wrappers (not spring roll)
peanut oil (for frying)

1. Place one wrapper in front of you turned at an angle like a diamond. Place three tablespoons of filling in the center.

2. Pull the corner closest to you up and over the filling. Fold in the corners at each side. While holding the sides in with your fingers, roll tightly forward with your thumbs. Seal with a dab of beaten egg. Set aside and repeat with the rest of the wrappers.

3. Heat two or three inches of oil in a large pan. Use tongs to turn the egg rolls. Fry two or three at a time until golden brown on all sides. Remove from the pan and drain on paper towels. Eat them while they're hot or double-fry following the directions below.

Double-Fry Technique (Optional)

Thick and chewy egg roll wrappers should be blistered from frying. Double-fry like Chinese restaurants do for an authentic texture.

1. After the first fry, refrigerate until completely cool. (If not serving in the near future, freeze the egg rolls in a plastic storage bag. Thaw before the second fry)

2. Fry a second time just before serving.

Serve hot with soy sauce and red dipping sauce.

RED DIPPING SAUCE

Egg rolls are often served with soy sauce, duck sauce or plum sauce. But in the Motor City you're guaranteed to find a plastic soufflé cup of bright red sauce inside your carry-out bag. Made from everyday ingredients, this economical sauce couldn't be easier.

1 cup water
¾ cup granulated sugar
½ cup white vinegar
2 tablespoons ketchup
1 teaspoon soy sauce
2 tablespoons cornstarch
a few drops of red food dye (optional)

1. Place the ingredients into a small saucepan. Whisk continuously and simmer until slightly thickened. Double the cornstarch for a thicker sauce.

ALMOND BONELESS CHICKEN
War Su Gai

Though the origin of Almond Boneless Chicken has been lost in time, many believe it was created in Detroit. Our appreciation for the dish is evident by the fact that 'ABC' is a staple offering of every Chinese restaurant in the area.

ABC features golden slices of battered chicken over gently wilted iceberg lettuce and jasmine rice. It's topped with brown sauce and garnished with toasted almonds and fresh scallions.

Velveting Marinade:
½ teaspoon salt
1 tablespoon cornstarch
1 tablespoon vegetable oil
1 egg white, whisked
4 chicken breasts (boneless, skinless)

Ever wonder how the meat in Chinese restaurant food stays so tender? It's because of a marinating technique called velveting. Use this marinade to tenderize any meat before you stir-fry.

1. So that the chicken cooks evenly, cover with plastic wrap and pound with a rolling pin until each piece has an even thickness.

2. Combine the marinade ingredients with the chicken breasts. Marinate for a maximum of twenty minutes in the refrigerator. (The meat will become mushy if left longer)

3. Rinse off the marinade and pat the chicken dry with a paper towel.

Batter:
3 tablespoons cornstarch
3 tablespoons all-purpose flour
½ teaspoon baking powder
1 egg, whisked
2 tablespoons water

1. Combine the batter ingredients and set aside.

Sauce:
1 tablespoon unsalted butter
1 cup mushrooms, sliced
1 tablespoon sherry
3 cups chicken stock
3 teaspoons soy sauce
dash of oyster sauce
¼ cup cornstarch (mixed with an equal amount of water)
salt, to taste

1. Melt the butter in a medium-sized sauce pan. Add the mushrooms and sauté for 5 minutes over medium-high heat. Pour in the sherry.

2. Stir in the chicken stock, soy sauce, oyster sauce, and cornstarch mixture.

3. Lower the heat and lightly simmer for 10 minutes. The sauce will reduce slightly. Taste and season with salt if needed.

Assembly:
peanut oil (for frying)
jasmine rice, prepared (for serving)
iceberg lettuce, chopped (for serving)
scallions, thinly sliced (for serving)
sliced almonds, toasted (for serving)

1. Heat ½-inch of oil in a large frying pan over medium-high heat.

2. Coat the chicken breasts with batter. Fry one or two at a time, for 5 to 7 minutes per side or until golden brown. Be careful not to overcrowd the pan.

3. Once the thickest part of each chicken breast reaches an internal temperature of 165°F, carefully remove and drain on a paper towel lined plate.

4. Cut the chicken into 1-inch wide strips.

To serve:
Spoon a layer of rice onto each plate. Top with the lettuce, then the chicken strips. Drizzle with the brown sauce and sprinkle with almonds and scallions. Offer soy sauce and extra brown sauce on the side.

WOO DIP HARR
Sweet and Sour Bacon-Wrapped Shrimp

This dish features bacon-wrapped shrimp and stir-fried onions tossed in sweet and sour sauce. It's topped with toasted almonds and fresh scallions. Woo Dip Harr is prevalent throughout southeast Michigan.

Sauce:*
¾ cup granulated sugar
⅔ cup water
⅓ cup white vinegar
¼ cup soy sauce
2 tablespoons cornstarch
2 tablespoons ketchup
¼ teaspoon salt
¼ teaspoon garlic powder
⅛ teaspoon ginger powder
⅛ teaspoon white pepper

1. Bring the sauce ingredients to a simmer in a medium-sized sauce pan. While whisking, cook until the sauce has slightly thickened.

*Or save time with prepared sweet and sour sauce.

Shrimp Prep:
16 jumbo shrimp, de-veined and butterflied
8 smoked bacon strips, cut in half
2 large eggs, beaten

1. Shell and de-vein the shrimp: Remove the shell from each shrimp, but leave the tail intact. With a small knife, make a shallow cut along its back to expose the dark vein. Place the knife tip just under the vein and pull it up and out.

2. Butterfly the shrimp: Cut a slit along the underside of the shrimp (Be careful not to cut all the way through). Lay the shrimp on its back and press its underside open. Cut a bit more if necessary.

3. Wrap half of a piece of bacon around each shrimp. Dip into the beaten egg and set aside.

WOO DIP HARR (cont'd)

Assembly:
peanut oil (for frying)
2 large yellow onions, cut into 2-inch pieces
jasmine rice, prepared (for serving)
sliced almonds, toasted
scallions, thinly sliced

1. Heat 1 tablespoon of oil in a large frying pan or wok. Over medium-high heat, stir-fry the onions just until they begin to soften, but are still somewhat firm. Remove from the pan and set aside.

2. Add another 2 tablespoons of oil to the pan. Sauté the shrimp until the bacon is cooked and the shrimp just starts to turn pink. *(Overcooked shrimp is rubbery.)*

3. Mix half of the sauce with the shrimp.

To serve:
Spoon a bed of rice onto each plate. Top with the onions and bacon-shrimp. Garnish with toasted almonds and scallions. Serve the rest of the sauce on the side.

CHINESE DINNER ROLLS

Fluffy and slightly sweet, these oversized yeast rolls are a local favorite. A technique called *Tangzhong* and a lengthy kneading time are the secret to these incredibly soft rolls.

Tangzhong:
1 cup liquid (can be milk, water or a blend of both)
⅓ cup all-purpose or bread flour

Dough:
5 cups all-purpose or bread flour
¾ cup granulated sugar
2½ teaspoon kosher salt
3½ teaspoons instant yeast
1 cup milk
2 large eggs
⅓ cup butter, melted
tangzhong (use all from above recipe)
½ cup milk (for milk wash)

1. First prepare the tangzhong. Mix the liquid and flour in a small saucepan. Simmer over medium-high heat while stirring constantly. Once it has thickened to a pudding-like consistency, remove from the heat and set aside to cool.

2. Combine the flour, sugar, salt, and instant yeast. Form an indentation in the center of the dry ingredients. Pour in the milk, eggs, butter, and tangzhong.

3. Mix with a wooden spoon until it forms a cohesive dough ball. Knead for about 10 minutes. If it's too sticky to knead, add just enough flour to make it easy to work with.

4. Shape the dough into a ball and place it into an oiled bowl. Cover with plastic wrap and let it rise in a warm place until double in size, about 45 minutes.

5. On a lightly floured surface, divide the dough into six uniform pieces. Cover the remaining pieces until ready to use.

6. Create layers. Use a rolling pin to flatten one piece into an oval shape. Fold both ends into the center so that the tips of the oval are touching. Again flatten with the rolling pin. (If at any point the dough is too stiff to roll out, let it rest for 10 minutes, then attempt again.)

7. Roll the dough into a spiral. With your thumbs, pull dough down from the top to cover its sides and to form it into more of a roll shape. Repeat with the rest of the pieces.

8. Preheat the oven to 375°F. Place the dough balls close together in an oiled pan. Let them rise again for one hour or until double in size. The sides should touch at this point.
(A 'pullman pan' will help to reach the authentic height of these rolls. They should be taller than they are wide. But you can still achieve close-enough results with a regular loaf or square pan.)

9. Brush the risen dough with milk. Bake in the preheated oven for 30 minutes. Remove once the tops are nicely browned. Let the rolls rest for 10 minutes before removing from the pan. Cool on a wire rack.

PEPPER STEAK

Pepper Steak originated in big cities, like Detroit, where Chinese immigrants settled early on.

Marinade:
2 tablespoons vegetable or peanut oil
1 tablespoon soy sauce
1 tablespoon cornstarch
½ teaspoon salt
1 pound beef steak (flank, sirloin, or round), fat removed and sliced into ½-inch strips

1. Combine the ingredients and marinate for 20 minutes in the refrigerator.

peanut oil (for frying)
2 large green bell peppers, sliced
1 large yellow onion, sliced
1 teaspoon minced garlic
1 teaspoon ginger, minced
2 tablespoons sherry (optional)
1 cup water
2 teaspoons soy sauce
1 teaspoon sugar
½ teaspoon salt
¼ teaspoon black pepper
2 tablespoons cornstarch
Jasmine rice, prepared (to serve)

1. Place 1 to 2 tablespoons of oil into a large frying pan over medium-high heat. Brown the beef and reserve in a clean bowl.

2. Add more oil if needed. Stir-fry the green peppers and onions just until tender. Remove from the pan and set aside.

3. Sauté the garlic and ginger until fragrant. Then add the sherry, water, soy sauce, sugar, salt, black pepper, and cornstarch. Whisk constantly and cook until thickened.

4. Return the beef, bell peppers, and onions to the pan and toss to coat with the sauce. Serve over white rice.

CHINESE ALMOND COOKIES

End your Chinatown feast on a sweet note with these classic Almond Cookies.

Makes four dozen

1 cup whole almonds, blanched
3 cups all-purpose flour
½ teaspoon baking soda
½ teaspoon salt
1 cup granulated sugar
1 cup lard (lard is traditional, but you may substitute unsalted butter.)
1 egg
1 tablespoon almond extract
1 egg yolk
1 teaspoon water

1. To blanch the almonds, boil for 2 minutes in a small pot of water. Drain and place into a bowl of cold water for a few minutes. Rub to remove the skins.

2. Combine the flour, baking soda, and salt in a bowl.

3. In another bowl, cream together the lard and sugar. Mix in the egg and almond extract.

4. Add the dry ingredients to the wet and mix until combined. Wrap the dough ball in plastic wrap and refrigerate for one hour.

5. Preheat the oven to 325°F (165°C) and line a baking sheet with parchment paper.

6. Pinch off pieces of dough and roll into 1-inch balls. Place each cookie two-inches apart on the baking sheet. Use the palm of your hand or the bottom of a glass to slightly flatten the balls.

7. Press one almond into the center of each cookie. Whisk together the egg yolk and water. Brush each cookie with egg.

8. Bake for 20-25 minutes, then remove from the oven. Let the cookies sit for 10 minutes. Transfer to a wire rack to cool completely.

UP-NORTH PASTIES

Throughout Michigan, and especially the Upper Peninsula, the pasty is a regional food of great pride. But its earliest mention can be found in Cornish texts from as far back as 1150 CE.[1]

During the nineteenth-century, America's mining industry was just developing. Highly-skilled miners from Cornwall, England arrived in search of better opportunities. The local miners learned a lot from the Cornish, like eating pasties for their midday meal.

They were filling, portable, and could be reheated on the end of a shovel held over an open flame. Eventually local Finns, Poles, Irish, Scots, French, Swedes, Germans, and Italians created variations that used their preferred ingredients.

It was common for entire families to work in the mines. But not everyone wanted the same pasty filling. To keep track, the family cook would stamp their initials into the dough.

Pastry:
3 cups all-purpose flour
½ teaspoon salt
1 cup (2 sticks) cold unsalted butter, cut into small pieces (substitute lard or shortening)
¼ to ½ cup ice cold water

1. For a tender and flaky crust keep everything cold and don't overwork the dough.

2. Using your fingers or a pastry blender, combine the flour, salt, and butter until it forms large crumbs. (or pulse together in a food processor)

3. Starting with ¼ cup, stir in (or pulse) the cold water with a fork until the mixture comes together in a ball. If it doesn't hold together, add a little more water at a time, until it does. Briefly work the dough to form a cohesive dough ball.

4. Wrap in plastic wrap and refrigerate for 1 hour.

PASTIES (cont'd)

Filling:
1½ pound sirloin beef (ground or chopped)
3 potatoes, diced
1 large onion, diced
1 small rutabaga, diced
¾ teaspoon salt
1 teaspoon black pepper
melted butter (for finishing)

1. While the dough is chilling, thoroughly combine the filling ingredients in a bowl. Refrigerate the raw mixture until ready to use.

2. Preheat the oven to 375°F.

3. Divide the chilled pastry dough into six equal pieces. Roll each ball into a ¼-inch thick circle.

4. Place ¾ to 1 cup of the filling onto half of each circle. Leave the edges uncovered.

5. Fold the dough over the filling and press the edges to seal. Roll the edges, crimp with your fingers, or press with fork tines for a decorative edge.

6. Transfer each pasty onto a baking sheet. Cut two or three small slits on top to release steam.

7. Bake for one hour. Check periodically so that they don't burn.

8. Remove from the oven and brush with the melted butter. Let cool for 15 minutes before serving. Enjoy!

1 History of the Pasty (accessed July 28, 2015); available from http://www.hu.mtu.edu/vup/pasty/history.htm.

PARADISE VALLEY
CHAPTER 4

B	lack history in Detroit reaches back to the eighteenth century. But in the nineteenth century, Detroit was one of the most anticipated stops on the Underground Railroad. For many it was the final stop before they reached the Canadian shore where slavery was prohibited.

The Underground Railroad was a secret network that helped runaway slaves. They usually made their way on foot, often at night, from one town to the next. Conductors of all backgrounds risked their lives to hide them in their homes, barns, cellars, shops, and churches.

Between 1820 and 1865, Michigan had around two-hundred Underground Railroad stops and at least seven known paths that led slaves directly into Canada. The Underground Railroad ran until the thirteenth Amendment abolished slavery at the conclusion of the Civil War. More than forty-five thousand slaves passed through Detroit to acheive true freedom.[1]

Forty-five years later, between 1910 and 1930, Detroit's black community started to expand. Beginning with 5,700 residents, the black population swelled to 120,000 people in just two decades. This was part of the "Great Migration", in which primarily black southerners sought a better life in the industrialized cities of the North.[2]

By 1920, nearly 80 percent of the city's black, male population was employed in mechanical and manufacturing jobs. They were highly industrialized. But when seeking housing they faced racism and discrimination.

Named for its rich topsoil, the Black Bottom neighborhood evolved as black residents needed a place for themselves. They were denied entry into most white neighborhoods, so much of the black population moved into the area. And with over three hundred fifty black-owned businesses, local entrepreneurs thrived at its peak in the twenties.

Soon another black neighborhood emerged nearby called Paradise Valley. From the 1930s to the 1950s, the area boomed with businesses, night clubs, and social establishments.

Paradise Valley was renowned for its contributions to American music, including blues, jazz, and big band. There one could enjoy a glamorous night out complete with fine dining and entertainment. The Paradise Theater, and other venues, hosted world-class musicians, like Ella Fitzgerald, Billie Holiday, Louis Armstrong, Dizzy Gillespie, and Duke Ellington.

While the entire city of Detroit lacked adequate housing, Black Bottom and Paradise Valley endured some of the poorest living conditions in the city. Rent was also sky-high, which forced many people to crowd together in single rooms. Too often these dwellings lacked cooking facilities and even indoor plumbing.

Officials didn't solve the housing crisis, but bulldozed the entire area to build the Interstate 75 freeway. Not only did the residents lose their homes, they lost their businesses and livelihoods as well.[3]

The Orchestra Hall, home of the Detroit Symphony Orchestra, is the original Paradise Theater.[4] Lafayette Park is where Black Bottom once stood and part of Ford Field, home of the Detroit Lions football team, was the site of Paradise Valley.[5]

1 "Encyclopedia Of Detroit," Underground Railroad, (accessed April 29, 2015); available from http://detroithistorical.org/learn/encyclopedia-of-detroit/underground-railroad.

2 "Great Migration," History.com, (accessed April 29, 2015); available from http://www.history.com/topics/black-history/great-migration.

3 "Detroit's Black Bottom and Paradise Valley Neighborhoods," Walter P. Reuther Library (accessed April 29, 2015); available from http://reuther.wayne.edu/node/8609.

4 "Orchestra Hall (Paradise Theatre), Detroit Michigan," Historic Structures (accessed April 29, 2015); available from http://www.historic-structures.com/mi/detroit/orchestra_hall_paradise_theater.php.

5 Krueger, Megan, "Black Bottom: Life before Lafayette Park," BLAC, (accessed September 4, 2015); available from http://www.blacdetroit.com/BLAC-Detroit/November-2013/Black-Bottom-Life-before-Lafayette-Park/.

BAKED MACARONI AND CHEESE

Cheese is part of our culture in the Midwest. So having a good mac and cheese recipe is a must. With tender pasta tossed in a velvety three-cheese sauce, this is that recipe.

But Detroit is also known for potato chips. In fact there were thirty-one potato chip manufacturers in the city at one time. Many cropped up in the twenties and thirties, like Better Made, which is now over eighty-five years old. Not only is this dish a celebration of cheese, but a tribute to our potato chip heritage.

1 pound (1 box) elbow macaroni or medium shells
3 tablespoons unsalted butter
1 small yellow onion, minced
1 teaspoon minced garlic
3 tablespoons all-purpose flour
3 cups half-and-half
1½ cups Gouda, Muenster, or Monterey Jack cheese, shredded or chopped
1½ cups Pinconning or sharp Cheddar cheese, shredded or chopped
1 cup grated parmesan-style cheese, divided in half
¼ teaspoon ground black pepper
⅛ teaspoon cayenne pepper
⅛ teaspoon nutmeg

Topping:
2 cups crushed potato chips
2 tablespoons unsalted butter

1. Prepare the pasta a few minutes less than it says to on its package. It's ready once it's al dente, or still a bit firm. Drain, but don't rinse. Set aside.

2. Preheat the oven to 350°F and butter a 3 to 4-quart baking dish.

3. Make the cheese sauce. Melt the butter in a saucepan, then cook the onions and garlic until translucent. Whisk in the flour and cook for a few more minutes. Whisk vigorously as you slowly add the half-and-half. Bring to a gentle simmer over medium heat.

4. Stir in the first two cheeses, half of the parmesan, black pepper, cayenne, and nutmeg. Cook until the cheese melts. Taste the sauce and season to taste. Mix in the pasta and pour it into the baking dish.

5. Combine the potato chips with the rest of the parmesan and sprinkle evenly over the top. Dot the topping with tiny pieces of the butter. Bake for 25 minutes or until the top is golden brown.

COLLARD GREENS

These collard greens are slow-cooked in a stock infused with smoked pork or turkey bones. So simple, yet loaded with flavor, these greens are the perfect side-dish.

8-ounces smoked turkey neck bones or wings (or 2 ham hocks)
1 teaspoon salt
1 teaspoon minced garlic
½ teaspoon black pepper
water
1 large bunch collard or other greens
1 tablespoon butter
1 tablespoon hot sauce

1. Place the smoked bones, salt, garlic, and black pepper into a large pot and cover with a few inches of water. Bring to a boil, then adjust the heat to medium-low. Cover and simmer the stock for two hours.

2. Remove the bones. When they're cool enough to handle, pick off any meat and add back to the stock. Throw away the bones. (Bone fragments can loosen, especially from ham hocks, which is why they are discarded.)

3. Wash the greens very well. Fold each leaf in half and cut off the thick stem. Chop into large pieces.

4. Add the greens, butter, and hot sauce to the pot. Stir occasionally. Cook uncovered for one more hour. Taste and season as needed.

BOOGALOO PORK SANDWICH
With Island Sauce

At one time, a place called Brothers Bar-B-Que served its loyal customers near the Renaissance Center. It was run by a woman named Jean, whose food is remembered so fondly that her fans still rave about it.

The Boogaloo sandwich is a particular source of nostalgia for many. It featured bell peppers, onions, and pork that were cooked on a flat-top grill until the meat was browned and slightly crispy. It was spooned onto a fresh bread roll with cheese, then finished with her "sauce of the islands".

Since Jean's original sauce recipe is a mystery, ours was developed only with clues left behind by her most enthusiastic guests. Hopefully it does her creation justice!

Makes four sandwiches

Island Sauce:
3 cups water
1 tablespoon cornstarch
2 cups ketchup
1 orange, juice
1 lemon, juice
1 lime, juice
1 teaspoon Worcestershire sauce
¼ cup brown sugar
1 tablespoon ground allspice
2 teaspoons ground cumin
1 teaspoon ground ginger
⅛ teaspoon cayenne pepper, more to taste
2 tablespoons unsalted butter

Assembly:
1 large yellow onion, sliced
pinch salt
1 teaspoon vegetable oil
1 pound pork, coarsely ground or chopped
1 green bell pepper, sliced
4 (6-inch) bread rolls
American cheese slices

1. Excluding the butter, whisk all of the sauce ingredients together in a saucepan. Gently simmer for 15 minutes. Whisk occasionally. Stir in the butter and set aside.

2. Place the onions into a small pot. Add enough water to cover and add a pinch of salt. Boil for 10 minutes. Drain and set aside.

3. Heat the vegetable oil in a frying pan over medium-high heat. Add the ground pork and break it apart with a spatula while it cooks. Stir in the bell peppers and boiled onions. Cook for a few more minutes. It's done when some of the pork has crispy brown edges and the peppers are soft.

4. Place two slices of American cheese onto each bun. Spoon the pork and vegetable mixture over the cheese. Pour some of the tangy sauce over everything. Enjoy!

BEER-BATTERED FRIED SHRIMP

At one time, there were several casual spots prized for their fried seafood, most notably crispy fried shrimp, that was sold by the pound. Dot and Etta's Shrimp Hut, Miley & Miley, Shrimp Shack, and other venues served local diners for decades. Sadly they are fading into obscurity, as one by one, they close their doors for good.

1 pound large shrimp, cleaned and de-veined
1 cup beer
1 cup all-purpose flour
½ teaspoon salt
vegetable oil (for frying)

1. Combine the beer, flour and salt. Refrigerate overnight if possible.

2. Pat the de-veined shrimp dry and place into a mixing bowl. Pour the batter over the shrimp and mix well to coat the shrimp evenly.

3. In a deep-fryer or a heavy-bottomed pot, heat the oil to 350°F.

4. One at a time, drop a few of the battered shrimp into the oil. Fry for about 3 minutes or until golden brown.

5. Remove the shrimp and place onto a paper towel lined plate. Serve with hot sauce or tangy rémoulade sauce.

FRIED CATFISH

Fried catfish is a southern delicacy, but it's also a popular dish in many of Detroit's soul food and barbecue restaurants. Around town, there are countless local fish markets that are happy to fry up your purchase on the spot. And due to the areas vast Catholic community, Fish Fry's are ongoing throughout the year.

4 catfish fillets (or cod, tilapia, or other white fish)
2 cups buttermilk (substitute 2 cups milk mixed with 1 tablespoon vinegar)
1 cup fine cornmeal
1 cup all-purpose flour
1½ teaspoons baking powder
1 teaspoon seafood seasoning (like Old Bay™) (optional)
1 teaspoon paprika
1 teaspoon granulated garlic
1 teaspoon salt
½ teaspoon black pepper
vegetable oil (for frying)

1. Place the fish fillets into a small baking dish. Pour the buttermilk over the fish coating both sides. Marinate in the refrigerator for at least one hour.

2. Remove each fillet from the buttermilk and allow the excess to drip off. Place onto a clean plate.

3. In another baking dish, combine the cornmeal, flour, baking powder, seafood seasoning, garlic, salt, and pepper. Press each fillet into the mixture. Coat both sides evenly and set aside (*or place the ingredients into a plastic freezer bag. Add one fillet at a time and shake to coat*).

4. Set the fillets onto a plate in a single layer. Refrigerate for at least 20 minutes.

5. Pour 1-inch of oil into a heavy or cast iron pan. Fry two fillets at a time for 3 minutes on each side or until golden brown.

6. Remove with a slotted spatula and place onto a paper towel lined plate. Serve hot.

*If frying a large quantity, preheat your oven to 250ºF. Place the fried catfish onto a wire rack with a drip-pan underneath. This will keep them warm while you finish frying. Leave the fillets uncovered so they stay crispy.

ONE-POT SMOTHERED PORK CHOPS

Though they're an old Louisiana tradition, smothered pork chops are a favorite comfort food served at most soul food restaurants in the Motor City.

4 pork chops
1 teaspoon salt
1 teaspoons granulated garlic
½ teaspoon black pepper
½ teaspoon paprika
½ cup all-purpose flour, divided
3 tablespoons vegetable oil
¼ cup unsalted butter
1 large onion, thinly sliced
1 cup mushrooms, sliced (optional)
2½ cups chicken stock (or water)

1. Rinse the pork chops and pat dry.

2. In a small bowl, combine the salt, garlic, pepper, paprika, and three tablespoons of the flour. Rub the seasoning onto both sides of the pork chops. Transfer to a plate and set aside.

3. Toast the rest of the flour in a large non-stick pan. Stir so that it browns evenly. Transfer the flour to a large bowl or pitcher and set aside.

4. In the same pan, add the vegetable oil and place over medium-high heat. Once the pan is very hot, brown the pork chops briefly on each side. Transfer to a clean plate and set aside.

5. Add the butter and the onions to the pan. Fry until the onions are browned at the edges. Stir in the mushrooms and cook until they turn brown.

6. Adjust the heat to medium-low. Stir the chicken stock into the toasted flour and pour the mixture into the pan. Stir.

7. Submerge the pork chops into the gravy. Cover with a lid and cook for 10 minutes or until fully cooked, but still tender. Taste the gravy and season as needed. If it's too thin, cook for a few minutes longer to reduce.

To Serve:
Plate a pork chop with some white rice. Top with the mushrooms, onions, and gravy. Serve with hot sauce.

BARBECUE RIBS

While several local gems, like Slows Bar B-Q, are renowned, Detroit's barbecue scene has always existed just below the surface. An extension of its southern roots, all types can be found here, from Memphis to Carolina style. Throughout the streets are endless wing spots, rib shacks, and big smokers that billow aromatic smoke in parking lots and empty fields. What it lacks in glamor, it makes up for with authenticity.

Dry Rub:
1 tablespoon brown sugar
2 teaspoons paprika
1 teaspoon ground cumin
1 teaspoon salt
1 teaspoon black pepper
½ teaspoon granulated garlic
½ teaspoon onion powder
¼ teaspoon cayenne pepper

Assembly:
1 slab pork ribs (full spare ribs or St. Louis cut ribs)
3 tablespoons vegetable oil
barbecue sauce

Special Equipment:
grill with a lid (or oven)
1 cup hickory or mesquite wood chips (optional)

*Cooking time: 4+ hours

1. First clean the ribs. Rinse with water and pat dry.

2. Next remove the membrane from the back side of the ribs. (This takes a little work, but gets easier with practice.) Start at one end and slide a knife between the membrane and the bones. Work the knife to pull the membrane away from the bones. Once you have one end pulled up, get a good grip on the membrane and pull it off. (A clean pair of pliers provides a strong grip.) If you can't remove it, slash through it with a knife between each bone.

3. Rub vegetable oil onto the ribs. Then rub half of the dry rub onto each side. Refrigerate for at least an hour or overnight.

4. Soak the wood chips in water for 30 minutes. Drain.

5. If using a charcoal or gas grill, heat it to a low temperature between 215°F-240°F. If using an oven, set the temperature to 225°F. If using a gas grill, use the wood chips according to your grills instructions, such as in a "smoker box". Or sprinkle the wood chips directly onto white hot coals of a charcoal grill. Do not use wood chips if baking in an oven.

6. Wrap the ribs meat-side up in thick foil. Place over indirect heat and close the lid. Cook for 2 hours.

7. Remove it from the foil and place the ribs onto the grill. Cook for another 2 hours. (More or less time is required depending on the size and type of ribs used)

8. Grab one side with tongs and bend the ribs upward and back down a couple times. If the meat appears to pull away from the bone, it's ready for the sauce. If not, cook for another hour and check again.

9. Brush on your favorite barbecue sauce or make your own. Grill for a final 10 minutes with the lid off. Serve with extra sauce and lots of napkins.

BRAISED OXTAILS OVER RICE

Though chefs and home cooks everywhere finally realize their value, oxtails have been a staple of soul food for ages. Cook low and slow for at least four hours to render luxuriously succulent meat with rich, beefy flavor.

2 tablespoons vegetable oil
3 pounds oxtails (seasoned with salt and black pepper)
1 medium yellow onion, chopped
1 green bell pepper, diced
2 ribs celery, chopped
1 teaspoon kosher salt
½ teaspoon ground black pepper
½ teaspoon paprika
2 teaspoons minced garlic
1 tablespoon tomato paste
4 cups beef stock
2 cups water
3 sprigs fresh thyme
1 bay leaf
white rice, prepared (for serving)

1. Heat the oil in a heavy pot over medium-high heat. Brown the oxtails and reserve on a clean plate.

2. Lower the heat to medium. Stir in the onions, bell peppers, celery, salt, and black pepper. Cook until the onions are translucent. Stir in the paprika, garlic, and tomato paste. Cook for a few more minutes.

3. Stir in the beef stock, water, fresh thyme and bay leaf. Loosen any brown bits stuck to the bottom of the pot with your spoon.

4. Return the oxtails to the pot. If needed, add enough water to cover the oxtails. Bring to a boil, then adjust the heat to medium-low. Cover and simmer for two hours.

5. Flip the oxtails over. Cook for two more hours or until fall-off-the-bone tender.

6. To thicken the sauce, first give everything a good stir so that nothing is stuck to the bottom. Increase the heat to medium-high. Simmer uncovered until it reduces slightly.
Or thicken with a cornstarch slurry. Mix a tablespoon of cornstarch with an equal amount of water. Whisk it into the oxtail broth and boil for a few minutes to thicken.

To serve: Place the oxtails onto a bed of white rice. Top with its flavorful sauce.

OLD FASHIONED BANANA PUDDING

Detroit's soul food restaurants make some of the best banana pudding around. This recipe is made the old fashioned way with real egg custard over sliced bananas. Make this in advance so that everything has time to soak up the fresh banana flavor.

Custard:
¾ cup granulated sugar
¼ teaspoon salt
2 cups half-and-half (or milk)
¼ cup cornstarch
3 egg yolks, whisked
1 teaspoon pure vanilla extract (or the seeds scraped from half of a vanilla bean)
2 tablespoons unsalted butter

Assembly:
1 box vanilla wafer cookies
4 bananas, sliced
whipped cream (Feel free to use the imitation 'whipped topping' found in the freezer section, but it's even better to whip real heavy cream with a pinch of sugar and a dash of vanilla until very thick.)

1. Whisk together the sugar, salt, and half-and-half in a heavy saucepan. Bring to a simmer, then immediately remove from the heat.

2. Whisk the cornstarch and egg yolks together in a bowl.

3. Pour ½ cup of the half-and-half into the yolk mixture and whisk well. Continue to whisk as you slowly incorporate another cup of the hot liquid.

4. Pour the mixture back into the pan. Whisk constantly and cook over medium-low heat until it thickens. When you lift your whisk, the custard should leave a thick coating. It will thicken further as it cools. Push through a fine mesh strainer for a smoother texture.

5. Assemble the banana pudding in a clear glass baking dish or trifle bowl. You may need to double this recipe to accommodate a larger dish. Alternate layers of vanilla wafers, sliced bananas, and custard. Repeat.

6. Once the hot custard has cooled, spread a thick layer of whipped cream over top. Refrigerate for at least 4 hours or overnight. Enjoy!

"DINTY MOORE®" SANDWICH
Corned Beef & Coleslaw on Rye

Hungry fans of corned beef are in luck when in the Motor City. Detroit is home to several world-class producers of corned beef including Sy Ginsberg, Jason Grobbel, and Tom Wigley, among others. Whether you favor the garlic-infused Jewish kind or the spicier Irish type, all styles are found here. Brisket's have been brined and seasoned in our city for over a century.

One of our unique contributions to the sandwich-scene is strangely titled the "Dinty Moore®" sandwich. It has no connection to the brand itself, and does not contain beef stew. It does, however, feature scrumptious layers of corned beef, coleslaw, Swiss cheese, and thousand island dressing on toasted rye.

Makes 1 sandwich

2 teaspoons butter or margarine
2 slices rye bread
2 slices Swiss cheese
4 ounces corned beef, thinly shaved
¼ cup coleslaw
lettuce (optional)
sliced tomatoes (optional)
pickles (optional)
1 tablespoon thousand island (or Russian dressing)

1. Spread a thin layer of butter onto both sides of two pieces of rye bread. Place one slice of bread into a non-stick frying pan over medium-high heat.

2. Build the sandwich on top of the toasting piece of bread. Start with the Swiss cheese, then add corned beef, coleslaw, optional vegetables, thousand island dressing, then one more layer of Swiss cheese. Cover with the other piece of bread. *If you want, make it a double or triple-decker!*

3. Support the sandwich with your other hand, then carefully flip the entire thing to toast the other side. Grill until the cheese is melted and the bread is golden brown. Slice in half and serve hot!

DOUBLE-BAKED RYE BREAD

Ever since Jack Goldberg and his wife Harriet opened the Stage Deli in the sixties, Detroit has enjoyed some of the best rye bread in the nation. The former army cook was determined to serve the freshest bread possible. So he began to order bread that was under-cooked. Twenty minutes before the lunch rush, Goldberg finished baking the loaves on site. The warm, crusty bread was sliced fresh for every order. His double-baked rye caught on and was soon the standard of local Jewish deli's.[1]

Preferment:
1 cup warm water
1 cup light rye flour
1 teaspoon instant or active dry yeast

Place the preferment ingredients into a non-reactive container that is at least double in size. Cover with plastic wrap and leave out at room temperature for 12 to 16 hours.

Dough:
2 cups warm water
1 batch preferment *(recipe above)*
1 tablespoon instant yeast
1 tablespoon kosher salt
1 tablespoon sugar
2 tablespoons caraway seeds, ground
2 cups light rye flour
4 cups bread flour or all-purpose flour
cornmeal (for baking)
boiling water (for baking)

Special Equipment:
spray bottle filled with water

1. In the order listed, place the ingredients into the bowl of an electric mixer (wet ingredients first, then dry). Mix with the dough hook attachment until it forms a dough ball. (If you don't have an electric mixer, mix the ingredients together with a wooden spoon in a large mixing bowl.)

2. Transfer to a large oiled bowl and cover with plastic wrap. Let rise in a warm area until double in size (one to two hours).

3. Divide the dough into two pieces. Shape into oval loaves and place onto a baking sheet that has been sprinkled with cornmeal.

4. Preheat the oven to 375°F. Place a pan of boiling water onto the bottom oven rack.

5. Loosely cover the dough with plastic wrap and let it rise for another hour.

6. With a very sharp knife, cut diagonal slashes (about ¾-inch deep) into each loaf.

7. Spray the loaves with water and bake for 10 minutes. Remove the pan of water from the oven. Bake for another 30 minutes or until golden brown.

8. Remove from the oven. Spray with water one more time. Transfer the loaves to a wire rack to cool.

To serve:
Warm for a few minutes in a preheated oven. Slice and enjoy!

1 David Sax. "The Search for Real Rye." The Atlantic. October 8, 2009. (accessed August 3, 2015); available from http://www.theatlantic.com/health/archive/2009/10/the-search-for-real-rye/27994/

NORTH AMERICAN PUMPERNICKEL

Traditional German pumpernickel is very dense because it contains a high ratio of rye flour. But in North America an entirely different tradition has emerged. Dark round loaves are crafted from a blend of wheat and rye flours which results in tender slices. Ingredients like coffee, molasses, and cocoa powder, provide its characteristic flavor and dark color.

2 cups lukewarm coffee
1 cup warm water
3 tablespoons molasses
1½ tablespoons caramel coloring *(optional – but essential for a truly dark loaf)*
1 tablespoon instant yeast
1 tablespoon kosher salt
1 tablespoon unsweetened cocoa powder
1 tablespoon caraway seeds, ground
2 cups light rye flour
4 cups bread flour or all-purpose flour
cornmeal (for baking)

Special Equipment:
spray bottle filled with water

1. In the order listed, place the ingredients into the bowl of an electric mixer (wet ingredients first, then dry). Mix with the dough hook attachment until it forms a dough ball. (If you don't have an electric mixer, mix the ingredients together with a wooden spoon in a large mixing bowl.)

2. Transfer to a large oiled bowl and cover with plastic wrap. Let rise in a warm location until double in size (one to two hours).

3. Divide the dough into two pieces. Shape into oval loaves and place onto a baking sheet that has been sprinkled with cornmeal.

4. Preheat the oven to 375°F. Loosely cover with plastic wrap and let it rise for another hour.

5. With a very sharp knife, cut diagonal slashes (about ¾-inch deep) into each loaf. Spray the loaves with water. Bake for 45 minutes or until the loaves sound hollow when tapped.

6. Remove from the oven. Spray with water one more time. Transfer the loaves onto a wire rack to cool.

DEARBORN
CHAPTER 5

Dearborn, which is surrounded by Detroit on three sides, was the home of Henry Ford. As the world headquarters of the Ford Motor Company, it grew into a thriving manufacturing hub.[1]

Today Dearborn has nearly ninety six thousand residents. Much of the population descends from nineteenth and twentieth-century immigrants from Europe or the Middle East. However, the Middle Eastern residents, who represent 40 percent of the population, are by far the most prominent. Many of which originate from Lebanon, Iraq, Syria, Palestine, and Yemen.

The first Middle Eastern settlers, who arrived in the early 1870s, were Lebanese. They sold produce, started businesses, and worked as autoworkers. As the population grew, so did the demand for authentic Arabic and other Middle Eastern foods.

Just across the street from Eastern Market, Gabriel Wadia opened the first Middle Eastern grocery in 1954. It became known as Gabriel's. Though it's changed hands many times, the market continues to import goods as Gabriel Import Co.[2]

But it was nearly fifteen years earlier, that Fadel Ganem opened the first Arabic restaurant in Michigan. His restaurant had no name, just a small window sign that read, "Arab food", written in Arabic script.

It was downtown in what was then a Syrian Maronite community. Primarily single men occupied the area and Ganem's food was both familiar and affordable.

Occasionally people from other cultural backgrounds would curiously wander in. Ganem's food was often their first experience with Middle Eastern cuisine of any kind.

He was forced to close during the Great Depression, and remained closed through most of WWII. But in 1944, he reopened just across from the original restaurant. This time his restaurant was designed for everyone to enjoy. It was launched with an English sign that read, *The Sheik: Syrian Food*" and was later renamed *The Sheik Café*.

At first he worked alone. Ganem cooked and diners casually helped themselves in the kitchen. As the restaurant gained a following, staff was hired and even his children washed dishes after school. Patrons were welcomed like family and often given tours of the kitchen.

In 1956, Ganem received an 'outstanding immigrant of the year' award from governor, G. Mennen Williams for introducing Arabic food to the people of Detroit. But he didn't just feed them, he also shared the warm hospitality of the Middle East.

With a modest estimate of three-hundred thousand residents, southeast Michigan is home to one of the largest and most diverse Middle Eastern communities in the world. It has the world's largest Chaldean population outside of Iraq estimated at 121,000. And Dearborn officially has the largest Lebanese American population in the country. As a result, Detroiters have access to some of the most authentic Middle Eastern cuisine in the nation.

1 Anan Ameri and Yvonne R. Lockwood, Arab Americans in Metro Detroit: A Pictorial History (Chicago, IL: Arcadia Pub., 2001).
2 Andrew Shryock and Nabeel Abraham, Arab Detroit from Margin to Mainstream (Detroit: Wayne State University Press, 2000).

TABBOULEH
Parsley and Bulgur Salad

Tabbouleh is loaded with finely chopped herbs, garden vegetables, and bulgur wheat. Add some to your sandwich, wrap, or pita to elevate your next lunch.

Salad:
¼ cup bulgur (cracked wheat)
¼ cup boiling water
2 bunches flat leaf parsley, chopped
¼ cup fresh mint, chopped
2 plum tomatoes, diced
½ red onion, diced (or sliced scallions)
1 cucumber, seeded and diced (optional)

Dressing:
¼ cup extra-virgin olive oil
¼ cup fresh lemon juice
ground black pepper, to taste
salt, to taste

1. Place the bulgur wheat into a small bowl (Use more than specified if you prefer a larger ratio of bulgur to parsley). Pour in an equal amount of boiling water and cover. Set aside.

2. Once the vegetables have been finely chopped, toss everything together in a large bowl.

3. Whisk the dressing ingredients together in a small bowl. Taste it and season as needed. Just before serving, toss the salad with enough dressing to coat.

FATTOUSH
Salad with Toasted Pita

Fattoush features romaine lettuce, seasonal vegetables, and crispy pieces of toasted pita bread. It's tossed with a zesty vinaigrette flavored by fresh lemons and tangy ground sumac.

Salad:
2 pieces of pita bread
1 head romaine lettuce, shredded
½ cup fresh parsley, chopped
¼ cup fresh mint, chopped
4 scallions, sliced
1 large cucumber, diced
2 plum tomatoes, sliced
1 green bell pepper, diced
¼ cup radishes, sliced

Dressing:
⅓ cup fresh lemon juice
½ cup extra-virgin olive oil
2 teaspoons minced garlic
½ teaspoon ground sumac
1 teaspoon kosher salt
freshly ground black pepper, to taste

1. Lightly toast the pita bread in an oven preheated to 350°F. Break it into pieces and set aside.

2. Prepare the salad vegetables and toss together in a large bowl.

3. Whisk the dressing ingredients together in a small bowl. Taste and season as needed.

4. Just before serving, toss the salad with just enough dressing to coat the salad.

HUMMUS
Chickpea and Sesame Dip

Hummus is the Arabic word for 'chickpeas'. Similar recipes have been discovered in ancient cookbooks from as far back as thirteenth-century Cairo. Scoop hummus with pita bread, tortilla chips, or fresh vegetables.

2 (16-ounce) cans (4 cups) cooked chickpeas, reserve juice
1 tablespoon extra-virgin olive oil
2 tablespoons fresh lemon juice
¼ cup tahini (sesame seed paste)
1 teaspoon granulated garlic
½ teaspoon ground cumin
salt, to taste
water (to thin)

Optional garnishes:
extra-virgin olive oil
cooked chickpeas
toasted sesame seeds
minced parsley
paprika

Special equipment:
food processor or blender

1. Reserve some of the chickpeas to use as garnish. Place the rest of the ingredients into a food processor or blender and process until smooth. Add water, a little at a time, until the hummus is very smooth.

2. Taste it and add more lemon juice, tahini, or salt as needed.

To serve:
Spread hummus onto a plate. Drizzle with some olive oil and top with garnishes. Serve with warm pita bread.

BABA GHANOUSH
Eggplant Dip

In Arabic, Baba Ghanouj means 'pampered papa'! We use our hummus recipe as the base for this delicious eggplant dip. But instead of chickpeas, it's made from slowly roasted eggplant.

1 large eggplant

1. Refer to the basic hummus recipe, but omit the chickpeas and instead use 1 large eggplant. (Variation: include one cup of cooked chickpeas along with the eggplant)

2. Preheat the oven to 400°F. Place the eggplant onto a lightly greased baking sheet. Use a fork to poke many holes in the eggplant's skin.

3. Turning occasionally, roast the eggplant for 40 minutes or until soft.

4. Remove from the oven. Place the eggplant in a large bowl of cold water. When the eggplant is cool, remove it from the water and peel off its skin.

5. Place the eggplant into a food processor along with the ingredients from the hummus recipe (excluding the chickpeas and water). Process until smooth. Serve with warm pita bread.

FALAFEL
With Tahini Sauce

A medley of aromatic spices, garden-fresh herbs, and crushed chickpeas are rolled into balls and fried. Falafel can be an appetizer or a main course. But it's a complete meal when served on warm pita bread with sliced tomatoes, onions, and lettuce.

Tahini Sauce:
½ cup tahini (sesame seed paste)
2 teaspoons minced garlic
¼ teaspoon salt
2 tablespoons extra-virgin olive oil
2 tablespoons fresh lemon juice

Falafel:
2 cups dried chickpeas (soaked overnight)
2 tablespoons all-purpose flour
1 teaspoon baking powder (dissolved into 1 tablespoon water)
1 small onion, roughly chopped
2 tablespoons fresh parsley
2 tablespoons fresh cilantro
3 teaspoons minced garlic
2 teaspoons ground cumin
2 teaspoons ground coriander
½ teaspoon ground ginger (optional)
1 teaspoon salt
½ teaspoon black pepper

Assembly:
vegetable oil (for frying)
pita bread, warmed
tomatoes, sliced
onion, sliced
lettuce, shredded

Special Equipment:
food processor

FALAFEL (cont'd)

1. To make tahini sauce, pour the ingredients into a food processor and process until smooth. Taste and season as needed. If it's too thick, add water, one teaspoon at a time, until thin enough to drizzle. Refrigerate until ready to use.

2. Place the dried chickpeas into a large container and cover with cold water. Let them soak overnight. They will double in size. Rinse the chickpeas and remove any that appear discolored.

3. Place the chickpeas, flour, baking powder, herbs, and spices into the food processor. Pulse until it's texture resembles course crumbs. (Be careful not to over-process. The falafel will become mushy, like hummus.)

4. Pour the mixture into a mixing bowl. Stir well and remove any large pieces that the food processor missed. Cover and refrigerate for at least one hour.

5. Shape into small balls or patties. In a deep frying pan, heat 1 to 2-inches of vegetable oil to 350°F. Fry the falafel until golden brown on all sides. Remove with tongs or a slotted spoon and drain on a paper towel lined plate.

To serve:
Place two or three falafel onto warm pita bread. Add fresh vegetables like tomatoes, sliced onions, cucumbers, and lettuce. Drizzle with tahini sauce.

MUJADARA
Lentils & Rice with Caramelized Onions

It's been said that a hungry man would sell his soul for a dish of mujadara. Meaning 'pockmarked', in Arabic, mujadara has been enjoyed for centuries. In fact the first known recipe was found in a cookbook from 1226 CE Iraq.

At one time, Mujadara that contained meat was a luxurious dish reserved for celebrations. While the common vegetarian type was consumed by the poor.

1 cup whole lentils, rinsed
2 cups water
¼ cup vegetable oil
4 yellow onions, sliced thin
2 cups chicken stock (or water)
1 cup long-grain white rice, rinsed (or bulgur wheat)
1 teaspoon ground cumin
1½ teaspoons salt
½ teaspoon black pepper
extra-virgin olive oil (for serving)
¼ cup fresh parsley, minced (to garnish)

1. Place the lentils and 2 cups of water into a small pot. Bring to a boil, then lower the heat and simmer for 15 minutes. Set aside.

2. Heat the vegetable oil in a medium-sized pan with a lid. Stir in the onions and sprinkle with a pinch of salt. Stirring frequently, slowly caramelize the onions over medium-low heat for at least 30 minutes. The onions should be well caramelized.

3. Stir 2 cups of chicken stock into the onions.

4. Stir in the lentils, rice, cumin, salt, and pepper. Turn up the heat and bring to a boil. Once it is boiling, reduce the heat to low and cover. Cook for 15 minutes.

5. After 15 minutes, taste the mujadara to confirm that both the lentils and rice are tender. Season with salt and pepper to taste.

To serve:
Drizzle with olive oil and garnish with parsley.

ZESTY CHICKEN GHALLABA
Chicken & Vegetables with Rice Pilaf

Though ghallaba is everyday comfort food in the Middle East, in America it's noticeably limited to restaurants in the Detroit area. It's almost always offered as 'classic' or 'zesty' style, and served over almond rice pilaf and sometimes hummus too.

Zesty Sauce:
1 tablespoon minced garlic
¼ cup extra-virgin olive oil
1 green chile or jalapeño, minced
¼ cup fresh lemon juice
2 teaspoons dried oregano
1 teaspoon ground cumin
1 teaspoon paprika

Almond Rice Pilaf:
1 tablespoon extra-virgin olive oil
1 cup basmati rice, rinse well
½ cup vermicelli (angel hair) pasta, broken into small pieces
2¼ cups chicken stock
½ teaspoon salt
¼ cup sliced almonds, toasted

Assembly:
2 tablespoons extra-virgin olive oil
1 pound chicken, diced
1 small yellow onion, diced
2 bell peppers, sliced (any color)
1 carrot, sliced thin
1 cup mushrooms, sliced
1 (14.5-ounce) can diced tomatoes
ground black pepper, to taste
salt, to taste
fresh parsley, minced (garnish)
ground sumac (garnish)
lemon wedges (garnish)

1. First prepare the 'zesty sauce'. In a small pot simmer the minced garlic in the olive oil for a few minutes over medium heat. Remove from the heat and pour into a small bowl. Whisk in the rest of the sauce ingredients.

2. Next start the rice pilaf. Heat 1 tablespoon of vegetable oil in a medium-sized pot with a lid. Stir in the broken pasta and rice. Cook until the pasta is golden-brown. Stir in the water and salt. Bring to a boil. Adjust the heat to low and cover. Cook for 20 minutes. Toss with the toasted almonds and reserve.

3. Make the ghallaba while the rice pilaf cooks. Heat the olive oil in a deep frying pan. Cook the chicken halfway over medium-high heat. Transfer the chicken to a bowl to finish later.

4. Stir in the onions, bell peppers, and carrot. Sauté over medium-high heat for about five minutes letting the vegetables brown a bit. Pour in the zesty sauce to deglaze the pan.

5. Stir in the mushrooms, tomatoes, and the partially cooked chicken. Simmer until the carrots are tender, the chicken is cooked, and the sauce has slightly reduced. Season to taste.

To serve:
Serve ghallaba with rice pilaf or hummus. Sprinkle with parsley and ground sumac. Garnish with lemon wedges.

CHICKEN SHAWARMA
with Toum Garlic Sauce

An immensely popular sandwich in Detroit, Chicken Shawarma contains succulent marinated chicken encased in a warm pita with fresh vegetables. It's drizzled with tahini sauce or a garlic sauce called *toum*. Though shawarma is traditionally roasted on a rotisserie grill, this recipe captures it's essence and is easy to make.

Marinade:
½ cup plain yogurt
2 tablespoons lemon juice
2 tablespoons apple cider vinegar
2 tablespoons extra-virgin olive oil
1 tablespoon minced garlic
1 teaspoon salt
1 teaspoon paprika
1 teaspoon ground cumin
1 teaspoon ground coriander
½ teaspoon ground cinnamon
½ teaspoon ground black pepper
2 pounds boneless skinless chicken breasts or thighs

Toum Garlic Sauce: (substitute mayonnaise or tahini sauce)
2 tablespoons minced garlic
pinch salt
¼ cup vegetable oil (light, neutral-flavored oil like sunflower or canola.)
1 lemon, juiced

Assembly:
vegetable oil (for frying)
pita bread, warmed
sliced tomatoes
shredded romaine lettuce

Extras:
cucumbers
onions
parsley
pickles
French fries

1. Whisk together the marinade ingredients. Slice the chicken into half-inch pieces and combine with the marinade. Cover and refrigerate for at least four hours or overnight.

2. Toum garlic sauce is an emulsion similar to mayonnaise. Using a mortar and pestle or small food processor, blend the garlic and salt. Alternating, add a small amount of oil, then some of the lemon. Slowly incorporate more of each, blending well before each addition. This is tricky, but if done right you'll have fluffy, creamy garlic spread.

3. Cook the chicken over direct heat so that the exterior is slightly charred, but the inside remains moist. Cook on a charcoal grill, broil, or pan-fry over medium-high heat until the thickest part reaches 165°F.

4. Cut the chicken into slices or shred it with two forks.

To serve:
Spread garlic sauce onto a warm pita. Top with grilled chicken and the accompaniments of your choice.

GRILLED KAFTA KABOBS
Spiced Meat on Skewers

Perfect for summer grilling, skewered meat is seasoned with fresh herbs and fragrant spices.

¼ **cup yellow onion, minced**
¼ **cup fresh parsley, minced**
1 **pound ground lamb or beef**
1 **tablespoon minced garlic**
2 **teaspoons ground coriander**
1 **teaspoon ground cumin**
1 **teaspoon salt**
½ **teaspoon ground allspice or ginger**
½ **teaspoon ground black pepper**
¼ **teaspoon cayenne pepper**

Special Equipment:
skewers (soak in water for 30 minutes if bamboo)
grill

1. After mincing, press the onion and parsley with paper towel to remove their moisture. Thoroughly combine the ground meat, onions, parsley, garlic, and spices.

2. Divide into eight portions. Press each portion around one end of a skewer to form a cigar-shaped cylinder that is approximately 1-inch thick. Cover and refrigerate the kebabs for at least one hour.

3. If using an outdoor grill, build a fire with charcoal for the best flavor. Or use the broiler in your oven. Turning occasionally with tongs, grill for 10 to 15 minutes or until the meat is cooked and lightly charred on all sides.

To serve:
Enjoy kafta on warm pita bread with fresh or grilled vegetables.

ASHTA FRUIT COCKTAIL
Fresh Fruit over Rose Scented Cream

Ashta, or Kashta, is a mildly sweetened cream delicately flavored with rose and orange blossom water. This luxurious cream often fills pastries and desserts. And it's also paired with fresh fruit to make this amazing fruit cocktail. Drizzle with honey and sprinkle with chopped pistachios for an elegant treat.

The traditional method of clotting cream is time-consuming and expensive. So chefs developed this modern version which is practical and every bit as delicious.

3 cups half-and-half
4 slices white bread, crusts removed and torn into small pieces
2 tablespoons corn starch
3 tablespoons granulated sugar
1 teaspoon rose water
1 teaspoon orange blossom water (optional)

Assembly:
banana, sliced
strawberries, sliced
honey
pistachios, chopped

1. Place the bread, half-and-half, cornstarch, and sugar into a sauce pan. While stirring continuously, simmer over medium heat until slightly thickened. Remove from the heat. It will thicken more as it cools.

2. Stir in the rose and orange blossom waters.

3. Set aside to cool for about 10 minutes then transfer to a clean container. Press plastic wrap directly onto the surface of the pudding to prevent a skin from forming. Refrigerate for at least two hours. Ashta is good for two to three days in the refrigerator.

To serve:
Briskly stir the cool ashta. Portion onto plates and top with bananas and strawberries. Drizzle with honey and sprinkle with chopped pistachios.

ZIPPY STEAKHOUSE SAUCE

Lelli's, who began serving Northern Italian cuisine on Woodward in 1939, is accredited with the initial creation of a similar sauce. A sauce that doesn't mask the flavor of steak, but enhances it. Because of its immense popularity, several local chefs have devised their own versions to keep up with demand. Adapted from various sources, this recipe brings steakhouse flavor into your kitchen.

4 steaks (perfect for filet mignon)
½ cup (one 4-ounce stick) unsalted butter (preferably clarified)
¼ cup Maggi® seasoning
2 tablespoons low-sodium soy sauce
2 tablespoons veal demi-glace or beef stock
pinch cayenne pepper

1. Take out a frying pan, a baking dish, and a small pot. Preheat the oven to 400°F.

2. Once the oven is fully heated, add a splash of oil to the frying pan and place over medium-high heat. Briefly sear the steaks until browned on both sides. Transfer to the baking dish.

3. In the same frying pan, melt the butter with the steak drippings. Whisk in the rest of the ingredients. Simmer for a minute, then turn off the heat. Strain and set aside.

4. Cook the steaks in the oven for a few minutes at a time until they are done to your liking. Drizzle about a tablespoon of sauce over each steak and serve.

DETROIT HONEY HOT WINGS

Though not much is known of their origin, hot wings named after the Motor City can't be a bad thing.

vegetable oil
2 pounds chicken wings (or chicken breasts cut into pieces)
¼ cup (2-ounces) unsalted butter, melted
¾ cup honey
½ cup sriracha or other hot sauce
salt

1. Preheat the oven to 375°F

2. In a heavy pot, heat about an inch of vegetable oil to 375°F

3. Fry half of the chicken wings until they are golden brown, about 5 minutes. Remove with a slotted spoon and drain on a paper towel lined plate. Fry the other half.

4. Melt the butter in a small saucepan. Stir in the honey and hot sauce. (Adjust the ratio of honey to hot sauce to suit your taste). Bring to a simmer, then turn off the heat. Taste and add salt if needed.

5. Transfer the wings to a baking dish. Pour on the honey hot sauce and toss to coat. Bake for 10 minutes.

HONEY GLAZED HAM

When Harry J. Hoenselaar opened the first Honey-Baked® Ham store in Michigan, he couldn't have known that his company would become the nation's oldest and largest specialty ham retailer. Today, there are more than four-hundred stores nationwide.

Inspired by this local success story, our recipe features succulent ham that's basted in a medley of fruit juices and spices. It's finished with a sweet brown sugar and honey glaze.

1 smoked ham (fully-cooked and spiral cut)
1 cup orange juice
1 cup pear nectar
1 cup apple cider
½ teaspoon ground ginger
¼ teaspoon ground cloves
1 tablespoon liquid smoke (optional)
½ cup firmly packed brown sugar
½ cup honey

Special Equipment:
small butane torch

1. Preheat the oven to 275°F. Remove the ham's packaging and the plastic button on its bone. Place the ham into a roasting pan.

2. Whisk together the fruit juice, spices, and liquid smoke if using. Pour over the ham.

3. Bake for approximately 15 minutes per pound or until its internal temperature reaches 140°F. Baste in the fruit juice every 30 minutes while cooking.

4. Remove the ham from the oven. Cover and let rest for 20 to 30 minutes.

5. Whisk together the brown sugar and honey. Spread it onto the ham. Briskly wave the butane flame over its surface to caramelize the crust.

GREEKTOWN
CHAPTER 6

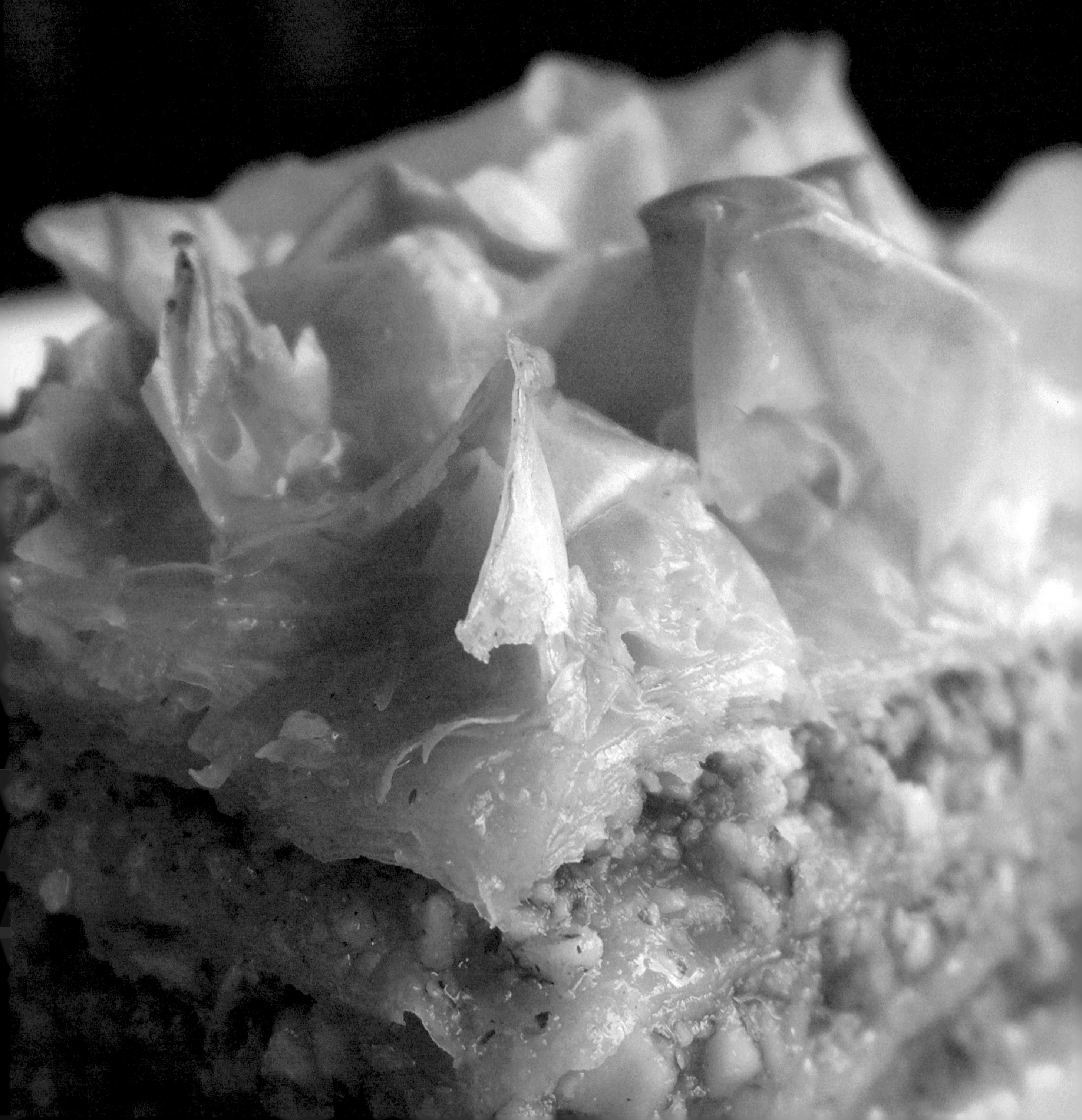

As the original German settlers moved further from the city, Greek immigrants began to inhabit the area known today as Greektown. Theodore Gerasimos, who arrived in 1890, was Detroit's first documented Greek immigrant. Others followed, and by 1909 there were two hundred fifty Greeks in the city. A few years later, the Christian Greek population suffered persecution and genocide, which prompted a mass exodus from their historic homeland.

It was during this time period that Henry Ford introduced his $5 a day job offer, which was nearly double the typical wage. This fueled a great wave of migration to the area. Detroit provided hope and opportunity at a time of devastation for so many.

They were quick to establish businesses in the neighborhood. The first of which was a Greek coffeehouse near the corner of Macomb Street and Randolph. Hundreds followed suit and opened cafés, restaurants, groceries, and boutiques. One of the first was Louis Perentis, who may have been Detroit's first Greek Millionaire.[1]

Eventually Greektown had become a commercial district with a dwindling amount of residential space. Though many Greeks moved on to the suburbs, their businesses remained.

During the sixties, more space was needed for institutional buildings and parking. To make room for the growing city, surrounding buildings were demolished, including the Greek Orthodox Church. Greektown was reduced to a single block. Local business owners realized their neighborhood was at serious risk. To save their investments, they joined together to promote the area as a Greek entertainment district. With the help of the Mayor's office, they revitalized what was left of the area. Additional street lighting was installed and the buildings were refurbished. They successfully promoted their shops and restaurants, breathing new life into the neighborhood.

Greektown's cultural identity was strengthened when the first Greek festival was held in 1966. The popular event continued for years until the turnout became too large to handle. But by that time, the area had firmly established its place as a must-visit destination, not just for locals, but also for tourists and out-of-town guests.

Sadly, after its peak the Greek character of the area has diminished. While at one time, it felt like a day-trip to Greece, just a few Greek restaurants are left. But the area remains popular for entertainment as the site of the Greektown Casino and many chain restaurants.[2]

The Greektown Historic District is one of the last surviving commercial streetscapes from the Victorian-era in Detroit. It was listed on the National Register of Historic Places in 1982. More than 120,000 people of Greek descent live in the Detroit area today.

1 Richard Bak, Detroit, 1900-1930, (Arcadia Publishing, 1999) 54.
2 "Allan Lengel, The Greektown We Knew Is Gone," Deadline Detroit, June 24th, 2012, available from http://www.deadlinedetroit.com/articles/929/the_greektown_we_knew_is_gone#.VgLP_isiiQ4.

GREEK SALAD WITH BEETS

Greek salad combines Mediterranean vegetables, feta cheese, and olives. But we go a step further with the addition of pickled beets. Beets were a staple food for many of the early settlers and also one of Michigan's top cash crops.

There is even an heirloom variety called the *Detroit Dark Red Beetroot*. Though it was actually developed in Ontario, Canada by a man known as "Mr. Reeves".[1] Nonetheless this resilient beet is considered to be one of the best. And for over one hundred years, it was the standard by which all other beets were judged.

Salad:
1 large head iceberg lettuce, torn into pieces
1 large red onion, thinly sliced
1½ cups cherry tomatoes, halved
1 cucumber, sliced
1 green bell pepper, sliced
1 cup feta cheese, diced or crumbled
½ cup pitted black olives
½ cup pickled beets, rinsed
whole pepperoncini (garnish)

Greek Dressing:
1 cup red wine vinegar
¾ cup extra-virgin olive oil
1½ teaspoons Dijon mustard
2 teaspoons dried oregano
2 teaspoons garlic powder
1 teaspoon onion powder
1 teaspoon dried parsley
1½ teaspoons black pepper
1 teaspoon salt

Creamy Pink Style:
½ cup mayonnaise
2 tablespoons pickled beet juice (from jar)

1Beet Seeds - 'Detroit Dark Red' Everwilde Farms, (accessed August 13, 2015); available from http://www.everwilde.com/store/Detroit-Dark-Red-Beet-Seeds.html.

1. Toss the vegetables in a large mixing bowl. To serve family style, layer the ingredients in a large serving bowl. Place the lettuce on the bottom and top with the remaining vegetables. Garnish with pepperoncini.

2. To make the dressing, place all of the ingredients into a cruet or jar. Add the mayonnaise and beet juice to make the creamy pink variation. Shake vigorously until well blended. Toss with the salad just before serving.

FLAMING CHEESE
Saganaki

Despite its Chicago origins, Saganaki has become a genuine Greektown tradition. After the cheese is fried, it's flambéed table-side as the server shouts "Opa!" The flame is smothered with a squeeze of fresh lemon.

1 pound Kasseri, Kefalotyri, or Pecorino Romano cheese
2 eggs
½ cup milk
1 cup all-purpose flour
¼ cup extra-virgin olive oil
2 tablespoons brandy
2 lemons, quartered
warm pita bread (for serving)

1. Cut the cheese into five-ounce pieces that are about a half-inch thick.

2. Whisk together the eggs and milk in a small bowl. Place the flour into another small bowl.

3. Dip the cheese into the egg mixture, then dredge in the flour. Shake off excess flour and set on a dry plate. Repeat with the rest of the cheese.

4. Place the oil into a small frying pan over medium heat. Once hot, fry each piece until golden brown on both sides.

5. While still in the pan, drizzle brandy over the cheese and light it with a match. Yell "Opa!"

6. Extinguish the flames with a squeeze of lemon and serve with warm pita bread.

STUFFED GRAPE LEAVES
Dolmathakia

These Dolmathakia are stuffed with rice, beef, fresh herbs, and a squeeze of lemon. Omit the meat and throw in some pine nuts for an authentic vegetarian version.

Filling:
⅓ cup extra-virgin olive oil
2 yellow onions, diced
1 cup uncooked white rice, rinsed
2 pounds lean ground beef
2 tablespoons fresh dill, minced
2 tablespoons fresh mint, minced
2 tablespoons fresh parsley, minced
1 teaspoon salt
½ teaspoon ground black pepper
1 lemon, juice only

Vegetarian:
Substitute beef with 1/2 cup toasted pine nuts

Assembly:
water
1 (8-ounce) jar grape leaves, rinsed
2 cups chicken stock
1½ lemons, juice only

1. Place 2 tablespoons of oil into a large pan and sauté the onions until translucent. Stir in the rice and cook for a few minutes. Place the mixture into a mixing bowl and set aside.

2. Add the rest of the oil to the pan. Brown the ground beef and remove the excess grease.

3. Combine the beef (or pine nuts if using), herbs, salt, pepper, and lemon juice, into the rice mixture. Reserve.

4. Boil a pot of water. Turn off the heat and add the grape leaves. After 3 minutes, remove the leaves and place into a bowl. Cover with cold water. Drain when the leaves have cooled.

5. To fill the grape leaves, place one leaf shiny side down. Scoop 2 tablespoons of filling onto the leaf near its stem. Fold in the sides and roll forward over the filling. Roll loosely so that the rice has room to expand.

6. In a heavy pot or dutch oven, arrange one layer of the rolls seam-side down. Cover with chicken stock and lemon juice. The liquid should come halfway up the rolls. Add more if needed.

7. Cover and simmer for 30-40 minutes over low heat. Serve as an appetizer or main course.

GYROS

In Greece, gyros are made from pieces of meat that are layered onto a vertical rotisserie grill. Some Greek restaurants in America still use the traditional method, but most use meat that has been compressed into loaves. Finely ground meat is compressed at 60 PSI. Then thin slices are shaved off as it browns on a rotisserie. Use this recipe to recreate the American-style gyros we love in Detroit.

1 pound ground lamb
1 pound ground beef
2 teaspoons dried oregano
1 teaspoon salt
1 teaspoon granulated garlic
1 teaspoon dried parsley (1 tablespoon fresh parsley)
1 teaspoon onion powder
1 teaspoon paprika
½ teaspoon ground black pepper
⅛ teaspoon cayenne pepper

Special equipment:
food processor
weight (to press the meat)

1. Preheat the oven to 325°F.

2. Purée the ground meat and spices in a food processor to make a fine paste – or mix well by hand if using finely ground meat.

3. Press the mixture into a loaf pan. Bake for 1 hour or until the internal temperature reaches 165°F.

4. Remove the pan from the oven and pour out the excess grease.

5. To achieve the characteristic density of authentic gyro meat, cool on a metal rack under a heavy weight (use a brick wrapped in tin foil or another loaf pan that contains something heavy, like soup cans). Then freeze or refrigerate until ready to use.

6. Just before serving, slice the gyro meat very thin. Pan fry or broil the slices on a parchment lined baking sheet for a few minutes.

To serve:
Serve hot gyro meat in a warm pita. Top with tzatziki sauce and sliced onions and tomatoes.

CUCUMBER YOGURT SAUCE
Tzatziki

This authentic Greek condiment is cool and refreshing. Serve tzatziki with gyro's, souvlaki, and dolmathakia.

1 medium cucumber, peeled
1 tablespoon extra-virgin olive oil
2 teaspoons red wine vinegar
½ teaspoon granulated garlic
1 tablespoon fresh dill, minced
2 cups Greek-style yogurt (or use regular plain yogurt - strain overnight to thicken)
salt, to taste

1. Slice the cucumber in half and scrape out the seeds with a spoon. Chop finely.

2. Place the cucumber into a a clean tea towel or layers of strong paper towel. Squeeze to release excess moisture into the towel.

3. Whisk together the olive oil, vinegar, garlic, and dill. Stir in the yogurt, cucumbers, and salt to taste. Refrigerate until ready to serve.

PITA BREAD

Pita bread is leavened flat bread used in Mediterranean, Balkan, and Middle Eastern cuisines. It can be round or oval in various sizes. Bake these from scratch to eat with hummus, souvlaki, or gyros. *(As well as falafel, shawarma, kafta, etc. from the previous chapter.)*

1½ cups warm water
2 teaspoons instant yeast
2 teaspoons kosher salt
1 teaspoon sugar
4 cups all-purpose flour
2 tablespoons olive oil

1. In a large bowl, mix the ingredients (excluding the olive oil) until they roughly form a dough ball.

2. Pour the oil over the dough. While still in the bowl, knead until smooth.

3. Cover the dough with plastic wrap. Move to a warm area and let it rise for one hour or until double in size. Punch it down and knead again for a few minutes.

4. Remove the upper oven racks. Preheat the oven to 475°F (250°C). Place a heavy-duty baking sheet or pizza stone onto the bottom shelf.

5. Divide the dough into ten balls. Cover with plastic wrap and let it rest for 10 minutes. On a lightly floured surface, roll each ball out to a ¼-inch thickness. The pitas will shrink a bit while baking.

6. Carefully place one of the dough circles onto the hot baking sheet. It should puff after about 2 minutes. Flip with a spatula or tongs and bake for one more minute.

7. Store the pita bread in a plastic bag at room temperature.

SOUVLAKI
Greek Skewered Meat

After marinating in a simple, yet vibrant blend of Greek flavors, skewered meat is cooked over an open flame. Make this recipe with beef, chicken, lamb, or pork. Enjoy Souvlaki on warm pita bread with sliced onions, tomatoes, and tzatziki sauce.

Marinade:
½ cup extra-virgin olive oil
½ cup white wine or white wine vinegar
1 lemon, juice and zest
1 teaspoon minced garlic
1 teaspoon dried oregano (or 1 tablespoon fresh)
1 teaspoon dried rosemary (or 1 tablespoon fresh)
1 teaspoon ground black pepper
2 teaspoons kosher salt

Assembly:
2 pounds boneless beef, chicken, lamb, or pork, cut into 1-inch cubes
2 large bell peppers, cut into 1-inch pieces
pita bread (for serving)
2 cups iceberg lettuce, shredded
1 red onion, sliced
1 tomato, sliced
tzatziki sauce (optional)

Special equipment:
skewers (or use thin rosemary branches to infuse with rosemary flavor as it cooks.)
grill (If you don't have a grill, broil in the oven.)

1. Combine the marinade ingredients in a container or large plastic freezer bag. Mix in the meat and peppers. Refrigerate for three hours or up to two days.

2. About half an hour before cooking, place the container of marinated meat and peppers onto the counter to bring to room temperature. Start the grill. If using wooden skewers, soak them for 10 to 30 minutes before assembling.

3. Prepare the lettuce, onion and tomato for serving.

4. Alternating, place the meat and peppers onto the skewers.

5. Grill until they are done to your taste. Place onto a serving platter and cover tightly with foil.

6. Toss the pita bread onto the grill just to soften.

To serve:
Spread warm pita bread with tzatziki and top with grilled meat, peppers and fresh vegetables.

CONEY DOGS

Constantine "Gust" Keros traveled to Detroit from Greece in 1903. While passing through New York City's Coney Island, he noticed that hot dogs were a booming business. He set out to improve the simple dog and began to experiment. His innovation was a natural-casing hot dog on a steamed bun, which was topped with chopped onions, yellow mustard, and his secret chili sauce.

Keros opened American Coney Island where he sold his dogs for a nickel. When his brother, William arrived, Keros taught him everything he knew about the Coney business. Eventually the store-front next door became available and William opened Lafayette Coney Island. Gust and William had a friendly rivalry, working side-by-side for over seventy years. Both restaurants are still run by family and are open 24-hours a day, seven days a week.

Inspired by his success, subsequent Greek restaurant owners also sold *Coney Dogs* along with traditional Greek items. During the sixties and seventies, several chains were established, including Kerby's Coney Island, Leo's Coney Island, Onassis Coney Island, and National Coney Island.

So what's in the sauce? Coney enthusiasts debate whether or not the original recipe contained tomatoes. But all agree that it never includes beans. And the intrinsic beefiness of the sauce can be attributed to the fact that Keros allegedly used mostly beef hearts. This recipe strives for authenticity and features a spice blend that is just right. Now you can eat Detroit Coney Dogs wherever you may be.

Coney Sauce:
1 tablespoon vegetable oil
1½ pounds coarsely ground beef heart or ground chuck *(finely ground beef may result in a gritty texture)*
1 teaspoon kosher salt
3 tablespoons unsalted butter
3 tablespoons all-purpose flour
2 cups beef stock
1 teaspoon yellow mustard
1½ teaspoons paprika
1 teaspoon onion powder
½ teaspoon granulated garlic
¾ teaspoon ground cumin
½ teaspoon turmeric
⅛ teaspoon ground cloves *(a pinch of cloves enhances the flavor of beef)*

CONEY DOGS (cont'd)

Assembly:
natural-casing hot dogs, grilled (not boiled)
hot dog buns, steamed
1 sweet Vidalia onion, diced
yellow mustard

1. In a heavy pot or Dutch oven, brown the ground beef in the vegetable oil over medium-high heat. Pour off excess grease.

2. Stir in the butter and sprinkle the flour over the beef. Mix well.

3. Whisk in the beef stock and stir in the spices. Cover the pot and simmer over medium-low heat for one hour. Stir occasionally to prevent sticking.

4. Blend for a few seconds with an immersion blender or food processor for a smooth texture. Don't over blend.

To serve:
Place the grilled hot dogs into steamed buns. Ladle a ridiculous amount of sauce over each dog. Top with yellow mustard and freshly chopped onions.

BAKLAVA

Within its paper-thin layers of buttery golden filo dough, spiced nuts are candied in a luxuriously sticky sauce of honey and lemon. Many argue about its origin, though it's believed that the ancient Assyrians made it in the eighth century BCE.[1]

Considering the magnitude of people with Mediterranean and Middle Eastern ancestry throughout southeast Michigan, it's no wonder that baklava can be found everywhere, from pizzerias to gas stations.

½ pound walnuts, chopped finely
½ pound pistachios, chopped finely
½ cup granulated sugar
1 teaspoon ground cinnamon (personalize your baklava with pinch of ground cloves, allspice, ginger or cardamom.)
1 (16 ounce) package filo dough (Thaw in the refrigerator overnight)
1 cup unsalted butter, melted

Honey syrup:
1 cup water
1 cup granulated sugar
½ cup honey
1 teaspoon lemon juice

1. Preheat the oven to 325°F and generously butter a rectangular baking dish.

2. Blend the nuts, sugar, and spices together in a mixing bowl.

3. Unroll the thawed filo dough. Cover it with a damp cloth or plastic wrap to prevent it from drying out while you work.

4. Place two sheets of dough into the bottom of the baking dish. Generously butter it with a basting brush or spoon. Top with two more sheets; then butter. Repeat until you have used 8 sheets.

5. Spread an even layer of the nut mixture. Top with two filo sheets. Butter. Then, add another layer of nuts. Repeat the process of layering with two sheets of filo, buttering and sprinkling nuts as many times as you'd like. Crumple a few of the layers to add texture.

6. Construct the top layer just like the bottom layer. Two sheets of filo dough, butter and repeat until you have used 6 to 8 sheets.

7. With a very sharp knife, slice the baklava into squares or cut at an angle to create diamond shapes. Do not cut all the way through. Leave just the bottom intact to help the baklava absorb the honey syrup as it cools.

8. Bake for about one hour or until the top is golden and crisp.

9. Prepare the honey syrup while it bakes. Bring the sugar and water to a boil in a small sauce pan. Stir in the honey. Lower the heat and simmer for twenty minutes. Stir in the lemon juice. Set aside.

10. Remove the baklava from the oven. Immediately pour the sauce over the baklava. Store the baklava at room temperature for several hours or overnight before serving. Loosely cover with foil when completely cool. (Covered baklava will become soggy)

To serve:
Place individual squares of baklava into small paper baking cups.

1 "What Is Baklava - History of Baklava," (accessed August 13, 2015); Available from http://www.habeeb.com/about.baklava.html.

CLASSIC SLIDERS

Many of Detroit's slider spots cropped up in the fifties and still feature their original décor of white tiles, metal counters, and spinning stools.

Here sliders aren't like the fast-food kind, and they're definitely not the trendy gourmet type. You'll never find them topped with crumbled blue cheese or micro-greens. They're greasy. They're crudely smashed as they cook. And they're a blue-collar staple that will always be at the heart of Detroit's food scene.

This recipe makes 8 mini-sliders. For larger sliders, divide the meat into 4 (4 ounce) portions and use regular sized buns.

1 pound lean ground beef
¼ teaspoon salt
½ teaspoon black pepper
2 large white onions, thinly sliced, sections separated
8 slices American cheese
8 small hamburger buns (substitute hot dog buns sliced in half)
yellow mustard (for serving)
dill pickle slices (for serving)

Special equipment:
metal spatula
large frying pan or flat-top grill

1. Mix the ground beef, salt, and black pepper. Divide it into eight (2-ounce) balls of equal size (four for large sliders). Press to flatten slightly. Don't worry about keeping the balls round. Detroit Sliders aren't meant to be pretty.

2. Lightly oil a large frying pan and bring the surface to medium heat. Working in two batches, place four beef patties at a time into the pan in close proximity.

3. Generously cover each patty with sliced onions. With the spatula, smack the onions flat into the beef, while at the same time smashing the patties even more.

SLIDERS (cont'd)

4. Slide the spatula under each onion-topped patty and flip. Top each patty with a slice of American cheese. Now on the bottom, the onions will cook the patty, and melt the cheese, with onion-infused steam. If the onions start to get crusty burnt edges, that's a good thing!

5. Prepare the buns. Flip only the bottom half so that both sides face down. Still stacked in this fashion, place both directly on top of the cheese. They're ready once the cheese is melted and the buns are steamed.

6. This part requires some finesse. But with practice, you'll be flipping sliders like a pro!
Slide the end of your spatula halfway under one slider. Support the top buns with your other hand. Now lift the slider from the pan. Remove the top bun and hold it underneath the spatula directly under the patty. Use your whole hand to support the top and bottom of the slider and slide it off of the spatula. Set it down right-side up. Repeat with the rest of the sliders.

To Serve:
Squirt on some yellow mustard and add pickles. Enjoy!

MEXICANTOWN
CHAPTER 7

Near the Ambassador Bridge, Mexicantown thrives with first, second, and third-generation Mexican Americans. Much of its Latino population descends from Jalisco, the Mexican state known for cowboys, mariachi music, and tequila.[1]

The first Mexicans arrived in the early 1900s, as Detroit was entering the industrial revolution. A large amount of laborers were needed to maintain the railways and work in the automotive plants. Sugar companies were also on the rise and recruited labor from Texas and Mexico.

By the late twenties, there were four-thousand Mexican immigrants in the area. Michigan was an escape from the political unrest of Mexico and the racism of Texas. By the thirties, there were nearly fifteen-thousand Mexican Americans pursuing the American dream in Detroit.

But when the Great Depression hit, everyone suffered. Michigan officials devised a plan to reserve local jobs for the people they perceived to be *American*. Instead of assisting Latino families, the Detroit welfare department, the federal government, and the Mexican Consulate collaborated to unjustly deport nearly two-million people of Mexican ancestry. Sixty percent of whom were legal residents or citizens. Detroit's Mexican population dropped sharply from fifteen-thousand to only twelve hundred.

Former Detroit residents, artists Diego Rivera and Frida Kalho enthusiastically supported the Mexican Repatriation campaign. But like so many others, they were misinformed. Supporters were led to believe that a better life, full of opportunity, was waiting for them in Mexico.

The Mexican government failed to follow through and many were stranded without housing or food. Eventually two experimental farming colonies were established with money raised by a Mexican charity.

The first group to occupy the colony in Hacienda El Coloso was from Detroit. They were not accustomed to the climate, living conditions, or the venomous wildlife native to the area. They also had no immunity to fight local viruses and diseases. Illness and death were rampant in the community.

During the forties, many survivors returned to Detroit to rebuild their lives. Over the next sixty years, there were mass waves of immigration and the Mexican American population grew.[2]

They settled around the streets, Bagley and Vernor. The community was called "La Bagley". Merchants sold Mexican products and services. And by 1969, the Holy Redeemer Roman Catholic Church held mass in Spanish.

The area was renamed "Mexicantown" as part of a public relations campaign in the eighties. It's now one of Detroit's most vibrant communities.

Today the area is renowned for its restaurants. People from all over commute downtown to dine at Xochimilco's, Armando's, Las Brisas, Mexican Village Restaurant, Taqueria El Naciemento, Los Altos, El Barzon, El Zocalo, Los Corrales, Los Galanes, and Taqueria Mi Pueblo. Tortillas are always fresh too, because local companies like La Michoacana, Hacienda, and La Jaliscience produce them for the region.[3] And its Cinco de Mayo parade attracts thousands of visitors annually as well.

Mexican food in Detroit is the product of two era's. Early dishes used local ingredients and conformed to local tastes. They used less spice, more cheese, and sometimes peculiar ingredients like green bell peppers and green olives. But recent waves of immigration have influenced the availability and demand for authentic Mexican food products. Both styles coexist in Mexicantown today.

1 "Exploring the Barrio." - Hour Detroit. (accessed April 29, 2015); available from http://www.hourdetroit.com/Hour-Detroit/August-2013/Exploring-the-Barrio/.
2 "History of Latinos in Michigan -A Decade of Mexican Repatriation." History of Latinos in Michigan., (accessed April 29, 2015); available from http://umich.edu/~ac213/student_projects07/repatriados/history/mihistory.html.
3 Dustin Block, "Michigan's Best: Detroit's La Jalisciense Tortilla Factory Is a 'natural' Choice for Tortillas," MLIVE, (accessed April 29, 2015); available from http://www.mlive.com/dining/index.ssf/2014/05/michigans_best_detroits_la_jal.html.

BOTANA PLATTER

One of Detroit's most celebrated dishes is the botana, created in 1975 by local restauranteur, James Galan. It's a solid example of early Mexican food. In fact its name simply means "appetizer" in Spanish. But here the botana is a specific dish – a nacho-style platter of tortilla chips smothered in refried beans, chorizo, toppings, and melted cheese.

Nacho bake:
½ cup chorizo sausage (optional)
1 (16-ounce) can refried beans
½ cup water
restaurant-style tortilla chips
2 cups Muenster cheese, chopped (substitute Monterey Jack or Provolone)

Fresh toppings:
1 tomato, diced
½ green bell pepper, diced
½ white onion, diced
½ cup sliced green olives
¼ cup sliced pickled jalapeños
1 avocado, diced
sour cream (for serving)

1. Preheat the oven to 350°F.

2. Brown the chorizo in a frying pan if. In the same pan, stir in the refried beans and water. Cook for a few minutes, then remove from the heat. Set aside.

3. Cover a large oven-safe platter with the tortilla chips. Top with the refried beans. Then cover with cheese.

4. Place the platter onto a large baking sheet and bake for 10 minutes or until the cheese melts.

5. Carefully remove the baking sheet from the oven. Sprinkle the rest of the fresh toppings over the hot chips. Serve hot with a side of sour cream.

CHILE RELLENOS

Chile Rellenos, which means "stuffed peppers" is an authentic Mexican specialty. Fried in a simple egg batter, mild green poblanos are filled with creamy melted cheese. Muenster is often used in the Midwest because it melts quickly and has a mild flavor.

4 poblano chiles
1 cup Muenster cheese, chopped
1 cup shredded Monterey Jack cheese
1 cup all-purpose flour
2 egg whites
pinch salt
pinch cream of tartar (substitute white vinegar or lemon juice)
2 egg yolks, whisked
vegetable oil (for frying)
salsa or ranchero sauce (for serving)

Special Equipment:
electric mixer

1. Preheat the oven broiler. Place the chiles onto a foil-lined baking sheet. Broil until their skins are blistered and charred. Carefully turn every so often.

2. Place the chiles into a large freezer bag or a bowl covered with plastic wrap. Let them steam for 15 minutes. Remove each chile and rub off as much skin as possible.

3. Don't remove the stems. Instead cut a 2-inch slit into the side of each chile. Carefully remove the seeds without tearing the peppers.

4. Combine the Muenster and Monterey jack. Stuff each chile with a half cup of cheese. Secure the openings with toothpicks if necessary.

5. Pour the flour onto a large plate. Roll each chile over the flour to coat.

6. Prepare the egg batter. Place the egg whites, salt, and cream of tartar into a very clean metal bowl. Whip to stiff peaks with an electric mixer. Gently fold the yolks into the whites until incorporated without loosing volume.

7. Heat 1-inch of vegetable oil in a deep frying pan over medium heat. Carefully dip the floured chiles into the egg batter, holding each by its stem. Place directly into the hot oil. Turn occasionally with tongs and fry until golden-brown on all sides. Serve with salsa or ranchero sauce.

POZOLE ROJO
Red Chile & Hominy Soup

Pozole is made from shredded meat and hominy simmered in a vibrant broth of puréed red chiles. It's finished with fresh vegetables and a squeeze of lemon or lime. It's eaten around the world and has one of the most fascinating histories of any food.

Since maize (hominy) was sacred to the Aztecs and other people of Mesoamerica, pozole was reserved for special occasions. According to the Universidad Nacional Autónoma de México and the National Institute of Anthropology and History, the meat used in pozole was originally human. During ritual sacrifices, they tore our the hearts of prisoners. Their bodies were chopped, then simmered with maize to make pozole. The entire community shared the soup as an act of religious communion.

When cannibalism was banned, pork became the traditional meat for pozole. The reason, according to a Spanish friar, was because it "tasted very similar".[1]

Today it's usually made with chicken or pork and their are red, green, and white versions. This restorative soup is also said to be an excellent hangover remedy.

Soup:
4 dried ancho chiles
4 dried guajillo chiles
4 dried pasilla chiles
boiling water (to rehydate the chiles) *(Substitute 1 (28-ounce) can of enchilada sauce for the chiles.)*
2 tablespoons vegetable oil
2 pounds boneless pork or chicken, cut into large cubes
(Or use an entire chicken or pork shoulder. Cut into large pieces, then brown in oil. Simmer the entire roast in the stock for a few extra hours than the recipe calls for. Pick the meat from the bones, then add to the soup.)
1 small onion, chopped
pinch salt
1 tablespoon minced garlic
2 quarts (8 cups) chicken stock
1 (29-ounce) can Mexican white hominy, strained and rinsed
1 bay leaf
1 tablespoon dried oregano (preferably Mexican)
1 teaspoon ground cumin
ground black pepper, to taste
salt, to taste

POZOLE (cont'd)

Garnish:
lemon and lime wedges
avocado, diced
cilantro, minced
white onion, diced
radishes, sliced
cabbage, sliced
fried tortilla strips
pork rinds *(chicharrón)*

1. First prepare the dried chiles. Remove the stems and the seeds. Tear into large strips. Toast the strips in a dry frying pan. Place the toasted chiles into a bowl and cover with boiling water. Let the chiles rehydrate in water for 15 minutes.

2. Heat the vegetable oil in a large soup pot. Brown the meat.

3. Stir in the onions, a pinch of salt, and a bit more vegetable oil if needed. Cook over medium-low heat until the onions are translucent.

4. Stir in the garlic, chicken stock, hominy, herbs, and spices. Scrape the bottom to loosen the flavorful bits stuck to the bottom.

5. Place the chiles into a blender along with 1 cup of its soaking water. Purée to form a smooth paste. Add more liquid if needed. Push through a fine mesh strainer.

6. Stir the chile paste into the soup. Simmer for 1 hour. Taste the soup and season with salt and pepper to taste.

To serve:
Ladle hot pozole into bowls. Serve with an assortment of fresh toppings.

1"The Pre-Hispanic Mexican Pozole Ate Human Flesh," La Crónica De Hoy, (accessed August 17, 2015); available from http://www.cronica.com.mx/notas/2007/317065.html.

SUPER WET BURRITO
Burrito Suizo

The Super Wet burrito is loaded with refried beans, seasoned ground beef, and fresh vegetables typical of American-style Mexican food. It's drowned in enchilada sauce, then topped with cheese and baked. In Mexico, a burrito topped with cream or melted cheese is called *Burrito Suizo*, which means Swiss burrito.

Filling:
1 (16-ounce) can refried beans
1½ pounds ground beef
1 small onion, chopped finely
1 teaspoon minced garlic
1 teaspoon ground cumin
1 teaspoon chili powder
½ teaspoon dried oregano
½ teaspoon salt
¼ teaspoon black pepper
1 cup shredded cheddar cheese
½ head iceburg lettuce, shredded
1 large tomato, diced
1 white onion, diced

Assembly:
4 large flour tortillas, warmed
1 (28-ounce) can enchilada sauce
2 cups shredded cheddar, Muenster, Monterey Jack, or Mexican blend

Extras:
iceburg lettuce, chopped
tomato, diced
white onion, diced
sliced jalapeno
sliced olives
salsa or pico de gallo
sour cream
hot sauce

SUPER WET BURRITO (cont'd)

1. Preheat the oven to 375° F.

2. Heat the refried beans in a small pot. Thin with some water so that the beans have a spreadable consistency. Set aside.

3. Brown the ground beef in a large frying pan. Drain off excess grease. Stir in the chopped onions, garlic, cumin, salt and pepper. Cook over medium heat until the onions are translucent. Reserve.

4. Warm the tortillas in a dry frying pan until soft. Spread a layer of beans in the center of each. Add the ground beef, then sprinkle with cheese, lettuce, tomatoes, and onions. Fold in the sides and roll tightly forward. Transfer the burritos seam-side down into a baking dish a few inches apart.

5. Warm the enchilada sauce in a small pot. Pour half of it over the burritos. Reserve the rest for serving.

6. Sprinkle with cheese, then bake for 15 minutes or until the cheese melts. Remove from the oven.

To serve:
Use a spatula to plate the hot burritos. Top with more sauce and desired toppings.

PUFFY SOFT SHELL TACOS

Though puffy tacos were created in San Antonio, Texas in 1978, Metro-Detroiters have come to appreciate them thanks to a local Tex-Mex restaurant chain.

Puffy Shell:
3 cups masa harina
1 teaspoon salt
2¼ cups warm water
vegetable oil or lard (for frying)

Assembly:
1 tablespoon vegetable oil
1 pound lean ground beef
1 teaspoon ground cumin
½ teaspoon chili powder
½ teaspoon granulated garlic
½ teaspoon salt
¼ teaspoon black pepper
1 cup lettuce, shredded
1 cup tomatoes, diced
1 cup shredded cheddar cheese

1. Combine the masa harina, salt, and warm water in a large mixing bowl. Roll the mixture into ping-pong sized balls.

2. Use a tortilla press lined with plastic wrap to press the dough into flat tortillas. If you don't have a tortilla press, cover a cutting board with plastic and roll each piece thin with a rolling pin.

3. Bring 2-inches of oil to 350°F in a deep and heavy pot. *(Caution: oil will ignite if too hot. Keep pets and children away when deep frying.)*

4. Drop one tortilla into the hot oil. Use a non-slotted metal spatula to douse it repeatedly with hot oil. It will begin to puff up. Flip it over. Press the spatula into the center of the tortilla to form a taco shape. Remove and place onto a paper towel lined plate to drain. Repeat with the remaining dough balls.

5. Heat 1 tablespoon of vegetable oil in a frying pan. Brown the beef with the seasonings.

To serve: Place one or two puffy tortilla shells onto a plate. Fill with seasoned beef and top with lettuce, tomatoes, and shredded cheddar.

AUTHENTIC PORK CARNITAS TACOS

Carnitas, which means "little meats" in Spanish, is slowly simmered with orange slices and seasonings until juicy and tender. It's then roasted until the edges are crispy and browned. Carnitas are delicious in tacos, burritos, tamales, and tortas.

2 pounds fatty boneless country-style pork ribs or pork shoulder meat, cut into 1-inch cubes (do not remove the fat)
2 tablespoons bacon grease, lard, or vegetable oil
1 tablespoon sweetened condensed milk (optional) *(It helps to crisp the meat)*
1 medium white onion, quartered
4 garlic cloves, peeled and smashed
1 orange, quartered
2 teaspoons dried oregano (preferably Mexican)
1 bay leaf
1 teaspoon black pepper
2 teaspoons salt
water

1. Place the ingredients into a large heavy-gauge pot. Add just enough water to cover the meat. Bring to a boil, then reduce to medium heat. Simmer for 2 hours. Stir and skim the top occasionally.

2. About 20 minutes before the pork has finished simmering, preheat the oven to 400°F. Turn off the heat when the meat is tender and the water has evaporated.

3. Throw away the orange slices and bay leaf. Transfer the pork to a baking dish. Shred the meat with two forks. Roast it in its own fat until its edges are crispy and browned.

To serve:
Scoop hot carnitas onto warm corn tortillas. Use two tortillas for each taco to prevent tearing. Top with pico de gallo, freshly chopped onions, cilantro, and a squeeze of lime.

TORTAS DE MILANESA
Milanese Sandwich

Milanesa refers to meat that is pounded thin, breaded, and fried, much like German *schnitzel*. It was introduced to South America by Italian immigrants. Somehow the *Tortas De Milanesa*, or Milanese sandwich, became a common menu item at Mexican restaurants in Southwest Detroit.

It's encased in fresh, crusty bread or Mexican bolillo rolls along with a myriad of fresh toppings. The toppings are of such significance that often bread is removed from the top piece to make room for more toppings.

Milanesa:
4 (4-ounce) boneless steaks, chicken breasts, or pork
1 cup all-purpose flour
1 teaspoon salt
2 eggs, whisked
1½ cups breadcrumbs
vegetable oil (for frying)

Assembly:
4 Mexican bolillos or French bread rolls
1 (16-ounce) can refried beans
2 cups lettuce, shredded
1 large tomato, sliced

Topping Ideas:
salsa or pico de gallo
guacamole
cheese
sour cream
avocado
onion
cilantro
jalapeños

TORTAS (cont'd)

1. Pound the steak or chicken to ¼-inch thick.

2. Prepare three bowls large enough for dredging. Fill one with flour, one with egg, and one with breadcrumbs.

3. Coat the meat with flour. Shake off the excess.

4. Then dip each filet into the egg. Allow the excess to drip back into the bowl when removing each piece.

5. Finally, coat each piece with the breadcrumbs. Press gently so that the crumbs stick to the fillets.

6. Heat a tablespoon of oil in a large frying pan. Roll the pan around to spread the oil. Cook two filets at a time over medium heat for about 5 minutes. Peek underneath the fillet. If it's starting to burn, lower the heat a bit. Flip over when golden brown. Cook until the meat is done to your liking. (Chicken must reach an internal temperature of 165°F. Pork must be between 145°F and 160°F.)

7. Remove each cutlet with a slotted spatula and drain on a paper towel lined plate.

To serve:
Slice the bread in half. Remove some of the bread from the top piece to make room for toppings. Spread refried beans onto the bottom, then top with the steak or chicken breast. Pile on your favorite toppings and enjoy!

FRIED ICE CREAM

Some believe the 1892 Chicago World's Fair is the origin of fried ice cream. Others credit Japanese tempura restaurants for its creation in the sixties. But in the early eighties, the restaurant chain, Chi-Chi's®, launched it as their signature dessert. It has become associated with Mexican food to the point that even some of Detroit's more authentic restaurants list it on their menus.

6 scoops ice cream
3 eggs, whisked
4 cups corn flakes, crushed *(variations: mix in dried coconut or chopped nuts)*
2 tablespoons granulated sugar
1 tablespoon cinnamon (preferably Saigon cinnamon)
vegetable oil (for frying)

1. Scoop six large balls of ice cream. Shape with your hands to make them as round as possible. Place onto a plate and freeze for 30 minutes.

2. Whisk the eggs in a small bowl. In another bowl, combine the crushed corn flakes, sugar, and cinnamon.

3. Use a spatula to loosen the frozen ice cream balls from the plate. Again coat the ice cream balls with egg, then toss with the cornflake mixture. Return to the plate and freeze for another 30 minutes. Repeat this process once or twice more to make a thick crust.

4. Heat the oil to 400°F in a heavy pot or deep fryer. Carefully place one ball into the oil and fry for one minute or until golden brown. With tongs or a slotted spoon, remove from the oil and drain on a paper towel lined plate. Repeat with the rest of the ice cream balls.

To serve:
Serve hot with whipped cream, chocolate, or caramel sauce!

D etroiters are passionate about Sicilian cannoli, Polish paczki, and even baklava, which has pre-Ottoman roots. But make no mistake, the Motor City has plenty of local creations to satisfy your sweet tooth. Here are a few ways to indulge like a Detroiter.

BOSTON COOLER

You may have heard that the Boston Cooler is named after Boston Boulevard, or the nearby Boston-Edison neighborhood, but neither existed at the time of its creation.

The mysterious milkshake* evolved from a drink called the Vernors Cream, in which dairy cream was poured into a glass of Vernors ginger ale. The Boston Cooler blends gingery Vernors with rich vanilla ice cream.

James Vernor created his signature ginger ale in 1866. For many years, the soda fountain at his pharmacy on Woodward Avenue was the only place one could enjoy it.[1] It's now the oldest surviving ginger ale brand in the United States. In 2011, March 13 was declared National Vernors Day. This date mirrors Detroit's area code 313.[2]

ginger ale (preferably Vernors™)
vanilla ice cream

1. Mix the ice cream with the ginger ale in a blender. Add more ice cream to make it thicker.

Some disagree on whether the Boston Cooler was a milkshake or a float (Vernors Float). The reality is that many locals did not experience the original at James Vernors soda fountain or any of the other retailers that later sold it. They made their own version at home. So make the Boston Cooler however you fondly remember it.

1 "Woody the Gnome - Detroit, MI." Enchanted America. July 5, 2014. (accessed July 29, 2015). available from https://enchantedamerica.wordpress.com/2014/07/05/woody-the-gnome-detroit-mi/.
2 "Encyclopedia Of Detroit." Vernor's Ginger Ale. Detroit Historical Society (accessed July 29, 2015). available from http://detroithistorical.org/learn/encyclopedia-of-detroit/vernors-ginger-ale

MACKINAC ISLAND FUDGE

Mackinac Island's fudge tradition began in the 1880s, when the Murdick family was commissioned to make canvas awnings for the Grand Hotel. Around that time, they also opened the islands first confectionery shop, Murdick's Candy Kitchen.[1]

With their mothers recipe, sons Jerome and Gould, made fudge in the front of the store. Ceiling fans wafted the scent of warm fudge onto the streets. Passersby were mesmerized, watching the fudge hand-crafted on marble slabs before their very eyes.

Today Mackinac Island is one of the most popular destinations for fudge in the United States. In the Fall, the annual fudge festival attracts fudge-enthusiasts, called 'fudgies'.[2] Approximately one million tourists visit each year.

Over thirty flavors of the rich confection are produced by competing fudge shops. Each guards their secret recipe carefully. Certainly one of the secrets to great-tasting fudge is the quality of its ingredients.

1½ cups half-and-half
4 ounces unsweetened chocolate squares
3 cups granulated sugar
2 tablespoons light corn syrup
pinch salt
3 tablespoons unsalted butter
1 teaspoon pure vanilla extract
½ cup chopped nuts or toffee bits (optional)

Special Equipment:
candy thermometer
putty knife or dough scraper

1 History Of Mackinac Island's Original Fudge Maker Original Murdick's Fudge. (accessed July 31, 2015). Available from http://www.originalmurdicksfudge.com/about-us/
2 Schedule of Events. Mackinac Island Fudge Festival. (accessed July 31, 2015). Available from http://www.mackinacisland.org/event/mackinac-island-fudge-festival/

1. In a heavy pan over low heat, cook the half-and-half and chocolate until it melts.

2. Stir in the sugar, corn syrup, and salt and bring to a boil. Without stirring, cook until the mixture reaches 235°F on a candy thermometer. This is known as the soft ball stage in candy making. When a teaspoon of the mixture is dropped into cold water a soft ball will form. Remove the pan from the heat.

3. Place the butter and vanilla into the pot, but do NOT stir it in. Let the mixture cool until it is lukewarm, around 110°F.

4. To finish the fudge, continuously stir with a wooden spoon (about 15 minutes), or an electric hand mixer, until the mixture looses its shiny appearance. Fold in the nuts if using. Spread it into a buttered loaf pan. Let it cool completely. Once it has set, cut the fudge into pieces.

(If you have a clean marble surface to work on, finish your fudge like a pro. Pour the mixture onto the surface. Use a wide putty knife or dough scraper to temper the fudge. Continuously turn over the fudge from the outside into the center. Cut into pieces when completely cool.)

HOT FUDGE DESSERT TOPPING

On June 17, 1875, Fred Sanders opened his first store with nothing but borrowed sugar and big dreams. Eventually his most illustrious shop, "The Pavilion of Sweets," opened on Woodward Avenue in 1891. Soon there were fifty-seven stores in the Great Lakes Region alone.

In 2002, another local chocolatier, Morley Candy Makers, Inc, purchased the Sanders brand and recipes to enhance its own chocolate legacy.

Today many of Sanders innovations have a cult following. And his shops were especially known for their hot fudge sundaes. The following recipe is adapted from the one released to The Detroit News by Fred Sanders himself in 1973.[1]

1 pound (16-ounces) baking caramels
½ pound (8-ounces) good-quality milk chocolate, chopped
⅓ cup milk
1 cup vanilla ice cream
1 teaspoon pure vanilla extract

1. First make a double boiler. Pour a few inches of water into a large pot and bring to a boil. Place a large metal mixing bowl on top of the pot.

2. Place the caramels, chocolate, and milk into the bowl. Whisk to combine as the caramel and chocolate melts.

3. Whisk in the ice cream and vanilla extract. Use right away or pour the fudge into a glass jar. Once the mixture cools, cover with a lid and refrigerate.

1 Kay Houston. "Of Soda Fountains and Ice Cream Parlors." The Detroit News, February 11, 1996, Michigan History sec. Available from

Almost All-Natural
BLUE MOON ICE CREAM

A blue churned enigma, the contents of Blue Moon ice cream continue to mystify all who have tried it. A handful of ice cream tycoons throughout Wisconsin and Michigan claim to have invented the flavor. What we do know, is that if you grew up in Michigan, the vibrant blue treat conjures pangs of nostalgia, whether you were a fan or not.

Blue Moon's flavor can be achieved with a surprisingly common lists of ingredients. As for that elusive mystery flavor, we believe cardomom is the secret. Many Scandinavians migrated to the Midwest and cardamom is a traditional ingredient in Scandanavian desserts. But the proof is in the *ice cream*. Let us know what you think!

3 cups half-and-half
¾ cup granulated sugar
1 tablespoon light corn syrup
1 teaspoon cardamom seeds (substitute ½ teaspoon ground cardamom or 1 tablespoon smashed whole cardamom pods)
zest of 1 lemon (substitute 1 teaspoon lemon extract)
zest of 1 orange (substitute 1 teaspoon orange extract)
pinch salt
2 egg yolks
1 teaspoon cornstarch
½ teaspoon pure vanilla extract
blue food coloring (optional)

1. Simmer the half-and-half, sugar, corn syrup, cardamom, citrus zest, and salt over medium-high heat. Remove from the heat once the foamy mixture begins to rise. Set the hot pan aside so that the natural ingredients can steep for at least 20 minutes.

2. In a bowl, whisk together the egg yolks and cornstarch.

3. To temper, whisk a half cup of the hot mixture into the egg. Whisk in another cup. Pour the contents back into the pan.

4. Gently simmer for a few minutes, then remove from the heat.

5. Whisk in the vanilla extract and a few drops of blue food coloring. Let it cool for 30 minutes. Strain. Discard the cardamom and citrus zest.

6. Pour into an ice cream maker and freeze according to the manufacturers instructions. If you don't have an ice cream machine, pour it into a metal container and place it into the freezer for one hour. Mix well every half an hour so that it freezes evenly. After a few times, let it freeze until firm.

Enjoy!

REFERENCES

Ameri Anan, and Yvonne R. Lockwood. *Arab Americans in Metro Detroit: A Pictorial History*. Chicago, IL: Arcadia Pub., 2001.

"Asian Americans in Metro Detroit, U.S." *Detroit Free Press*. Accessed April 29, 2015.

Bak, Richard. *Detroit, 1900-1930*. Arcadia Publishing, 1999. 54.

"Beet Seeds - 'Detroit Dark Red'" *Everwilde Farms*. Accessed August 13, 2015. http://www.everwilde.com/store/Detroit-Dark-Red-Beet-Seeds.html.

"Polish Americans in Michigan." *Bentley Historical Library | University of Michigan*. Accessed April 29, 2015. http://bentley.umich.edu/legacy-support/poles/.

Block, Dustin. "Michigan's Best: Detroit's La Jalisciense Tortilla Factory Is a 'natural' Choice for Tortillas." *MLIVE*. Accessed April 29, 2015. http://www.mlive.com/dining/index.ssf/2014/05/michigans_best_detroits_la_jal.html.

"Cherry Industry." Traverse City. Accessed July 9, 2015. http://www.traversecity.com/area/about-traverse-city/cherry-industry/.

Delicato, Armando. *Italians in Detroit*. Charleston, SC: Arcadia, 2005.

"Detroit's Black Bottom and Paradise Valley Neighborhoods." Walter P. Reuther Library. Accessed April 29, 2015. http://reuther.wayne.edu/node/8609.

"Encyclopedia Of Detroit." Underground Railroad. Accessed September 4, 2015. http://detroithistorical.org/learn/encyclopedia-of-detroit/underground-railroad.

"Encyclopedia Of Detroit." Vernor's Ginger Ale. Accessed July 29, 2015. http://detroithistorical.org/learn/encyclopedia-of-detroit/vernors-ginger-ale.

"Exploring the Barrio." *Hour Detroit*. Accessed April 29, 2015. http://www.hourdetroit.com/Hour-Detroit/August-2013/Exploring-the-Barrio/

"Great Migration." History.com. Accessed April 29, 2015. http://www.history.com/topics/black-history/great-migration.

"History of Latinos in Michigan -A Decade of Mexican Repatriation." History of Latinos in Michigan. Accessed April 29, 2015. http://umich.edu/~ac213/student_projects07/repatriados/history/mihistory.html .

"History of Mackinac Island's Original Fudge Maker – Original Murdick's Fudge." Original Murdicks Fudge. Accessed September 9, 2015. http://www.originalmurdicksfudge.com/about-us/.

"History of the Pasty." History of the Pasty. Accessed July 28, 2015. http://www.hu.mtu.edu/vup/pasty/history.htm.

"History." Roma Café. Accessed April 29, 2015. http://www.romacafe.com/History .

Houston, Kay. "Of Soda Fountains and Ice Cream Parlors." *The Detroit News*, February 11, 1996, Michigan History sec.

"The Kowalski Story." The Kowalski Story. Accessed September 4, 2015. http://www.kowality.com/category-s/124.htm.

Krueger, Megan. "Black Bottom: Life before Lafayette Park." *BLAC*. Accessed September 4, 2015. http://www.blacdetroit.com/BLAC-Detroit/November-2013/Black-Bottom-Life-before-Lafayette-Park/.

Lengel, Allan. "The Greektown We Knew Is Gone." *Deadline Detroit*. Accessed April 29, 2015. http://www.deadlinedetroit.com/articles/929/the_greektown_we_knew_is_gone .

"The "Little Italies" of Michigan." Jovina Cooks Italian. May 10, 2013. Accessed April 29, 2015. http://jovinacooksitalian.com/2013/05/10/the-little-italies-of-michigan/ .

"Meats and Poultry." In *Cookbook of the Woman's Educational Club*, 49. Toledo, OH, 1914.

"Michigan Apples." - Pure Michigan Travel. Accessed July 9, 2015. http://www.michigan.org/hot-spots/michigan-apples/.

"Michigan Maple Syrup Facts." Michigan Maple Syrup Facts. Accessed July 9, 2015. http://www.michiganagriculture.com/foods/michigan-maple-syrup/.

"Native Wild Rice Coalition." Native Wild Rice. Accessed September 28, 2015. http://www.nativewildricecoalition.com/native-wild-rice-coalition.html.

"Orchestra Hall (Paradise Theatre), Detroit Michigan." Historic Structures. Accessed April 29, 2015.
http://www.historicstructures.com/mi/detroit/orchestra_hall_paradise_theater.php.

"The Pre-Hispanic Mexican Pozole Ate Human Flesh." *La Crónica De Hoy*. Accessed August 17, 2015. http://www.cronica.com.mx/notas/2007/317065.html .

Sax, David. "The Search for Real Rye." *The Atlantic*. October 8, 2009. Accessed August 3, 2015. http://www.theatlantic.com/health/archive/2009/10/the-search-for-real-rye/27994/ .

"Schedule of Events." Mackinac Island Fudge Festival. Accessed July 31, 2015. http://www.mackinacisland.org/event/mackinac-island-fudge-festival/ .

Shryock, Andrew, and Nabeel Abraham. *Arab Detroit from Margin to Mainstream*. Detroit: Wayne State University Press, 2000.

United States. National Park Service. "St. Albertus Catholic Church." National Parks Service. Accessed September 4, 2015. http://www.nps.gov/nr/travel/detroit/d9.htm.

"What Is Baklava - History of Baklava." Habeeb.com. Accessed August 13, 2015. http://www.habeeb.com/about.baklava.html.

"Wild Rice Mounts a Comeback for Culture and Ecology." Great Lakes Echo. August 8, 2013. Accessed September 25, 2015. http://greatlakesecho.org/2013/08/08/wild-rice-mounts-a-comeback-for-culture-and-ecology/.

Woodford, Arthur M. "*A City of Many Tongues*." In This Is Detroit, 1701-2001, 186. Detroit: Wayne State University Press, 2001.

"Woody the Gnome - Detroit, MI." Enchanted America. July 5, 2014. Accessed July 29, 2015. https://enchantedamerica.wordpress.com/2014/07/05/woody-the-gnome-detroit-mi/.

"World Records." World Records. Accessed July 9, 2015. http://www.controlled-demolition.com/world-records.

Zia, Helen. Asian American Dreams: *The Emergence of an American People*. New York: Farrar, Straus, and Giroux, 2001.

Zuzindlak, Chelsea. Accessed April 29, 2015. Http://www.detroitchinatown.org.

INDEX